THE INSTANT ECONOMIST

The Instant

Economist

JOHN CHARLES POOL

ROSS M. LAROE

♦♦ **Addison-Wesley Publishing Company, Inc.**
Reading, Massachusetts · Menlo Park, California
Don Mills, Ontario · Wokingham, England · Amsterdam
Sydney · Singapore · Tokyo · Mexico City · Bogota
Santiago · San Juan

"A Missouri Fable" by John Ciardi (p. 58) copyright Rutgers the State Univ., 1962. Reprinted by permission of the author.

Library of Congress Cataloging in Publication Data

Pool, John Charles.
   The instant economist.

   Bibliography: p.
   1. Economics. I. LaRoe, Ross M. II. Title.
HB171.P69 1985   330'.024658   84–24568
ISBN 0–201–16884–7

Cover design by Marshall Henrichs.
Text design by Joyce C. Weston.
Set in 11-point Bookman Light by Modern Graphics Inc.

ISBN 0–201–16884–7

ABCDEFGHIJ–AL–8765

First printing, January 1985

To our most enthusiastic supporters:
Betty, Mike, and Laura Linda
Karen, Joe, Lee, and Bob
and, of course, Joven

ACKNOWLEDGMENTS

We gratefully acknowledge the efforts of the numerous students and practicing managers who took time to review and comment on earlier drafts of the manuscript. We especially appreciated the thoughtful critiques of, among many, Skip Beaver and Ted Colucci at Chase Lincoln First Bank, James Carnall of Eastman Kodak, Steve Lansing and Michael Wierzbicki of the Xerox Corporation, Leonard DeWeerdt of Hartman Allis-Chalmers, David Brown of Rochester Products (GM), Robert Butler of the Rochester Business Institute, Robert Tinney of Rochester Telephone, Susan Gatten of Harding Foods, Mary Jane Fisher of *U.S.A. Today*, and John LaRoe of the *Kansas City Times.*

We also wish to thank Professors Stephen C. Stamos, Jr. and Frank Slavik of Bucknell University, Ivan Weinel of Bradley University, Philip S. Thomas and Frederick R. Strobel of Kalamazoo College, Raymond E. Alie of Western Michigan University, and Martin Naparsteck of Empire State College (SUNY) for their thoughtful comments and assistance.

Finally, we wish to thank Carol Calacterra, Xarifa Greenquist, and Kalia Westerman for their assistance in proofreading various portions of the manuscript.

We, of course, are responsible for the errors and omissions which undoubtedly remain.

To our professional colleagues who will, we imagine, point out the many details and elaborations that were omitted, we would remind you that some decisions are best tested in the marketplace.

JCP

RML

I had just finished my MBA and was getting ready to go to work in management. One day I was talking to my father about his company. After a few minutes, he was shaking his head.

"You don't really understand the first thing about real economics."

"But I did well in all my classes in business school . . . ," I protested.

"Doesn't mean a thing," he said. "All they teach you about economics in school is the math. A manager needs to understand the basic sense of economics, because you can't be a good manager unless you're a good planner, and you can't be a good planner if you don't understand how the economy is going to affect your firm.

"Here," he said, writing something down on a piece of paper. "I want you to see this man at the university. He's an old professor of mine from graduate school. Tell him to explain what a manager needs to know about economics. Tell him it won't take much of his time . . ."

1
What Every Manager Needs to Know about Macroeconomics

The building was brick, covered with ivy. I wasn't surprised. The stairs took me quickly to the second floor. "Number two-fourteen, in Gleason Hall," my father had told me.

Mr. Marshall, the sign said. The door was closed. I knocked, feeling a little silly, but determined to get this done, even if it had been my father's idea.

"Come in," a rather soft voice said. "What can I do for you, Mr. Smith?"

The office was almost spartan—a couch, a few chairs, a couple of bookcases, and a few books: Adam Smith's *Wealth of Nations,* Karl Marx's *Das Kapital,* John Maynard Keynes's *General Theory.* Most of the rest seemed to be about mathematics. He sat behind a rather imposing desk, next to what appeared to be a computer terminal, fiddling with a pipe. That part I had expected. The TV in the corner I had not.

"My father was a student of yours, sir. Perhaps you remember him. James Smith, class of '53?"

"Yes, indeed," he nodded. "He was one of my top students. He's done pretty well in the game of business, hasn't he?"

"Yes, sir. He is the president of Abbot and Pierce."

"I know," he said. "So, what can I do for you?"

"Well, sir, I've just finished my MBA and I'm about to start my first job, as a manager, I hope. But my father thinks I don't know enough about economics. So he sent me to see you. He said it wouldn't take much of your time. So what I want to ask you, sir, is this: What does a manager need to know about economics?"

He looked amused. "Didn't you study it in school?"

"Well, yes. And I did quite well in my classes," I replied, beginning to feel a bit uncomfortable. "But my father doesn't think I learned much about economics. He says that all they taught me was mathematics."

"Well, you probably learned the mathematics of economics and not the meaning of economics itself. It's easy to lose sight of the forest for the trees. So, your father is right. A good manager can't get by without a basic understanding of what economics is all about." He paused for a moment and then asked, "Have you got something to write on?"

"Yes, sir," I said, taking out a yellow pad.

"Now, don't write anything down unless I tell you to," he said, rather firmly, but in a friendly way. "There are three different areas of economics a manager should understand. One is macro, another is micro, and the last is international. Write that down."

THERE ARE THREE AREAS OF

ECONOMICS

EVERY MANAGER SHOULD UNDERSTAND:

MACRO, MICRO, AND INTERNATIONAL.

"And," he said, "you can't really understand any one of them without understanding the others." Then he put his feet on the desk and stared at the ceiling.

"Let's start," he said, "with macroeconomics. In a

way, it's the easiest to understand. That may be because macroeconomic problems are splashed all over the front pages of the newspapers and get a lot of TV coverage. *The* issues in macroeconomics are inflation and unemployment. Macro is concerned with the overall level of economic activity." Saying that, he stopped a moment to ponder his pipe.

"Keynes, John Maynard Keynes, is the father of modern macroeconomic theory. His book, *The General Theory*, is over on that shelf. Do you see it? It's the one with the yellow and black dust jacket." As I started to nod, he said, "Get it and read me the first chapter."

Much to my surprise, the first chapter was only one page long. Clearing my throat, I read:

> I have called this book the *General Theory of Employment, Interest, and Money,* placing the emphasis on the prefix *general.* The object of such a title is to contrast the character of my arguments and conclusions with those of the *classical* theory of the subject, upon which I was brought up and which dominates the economic thought, both practical and theoretical, of the governing and academic classes of this generation, as it has for a hundred years past. I shall argue that the postulates of the classical theory are applicable to a special case only and not to the general case, the situation which it assumes being a limiting point of the possible positions of equilibrium. Moreover, the characteristics of the special case assumed by the classical theory happen not to be those of the economic society in which we actually live, with the result that its teaching is misleading and disastrous if we attempt to apply it to the facts of experience.

"I guess," I said, "that if I understood which is the general case and which is the special case I could figure out what he was saying."

"You're right. That is, indeed, the problem," Professor Marshall said. And with that, he put down his pipe and leaned forward in his chair.

"You see," he said, "when Keynes wrote, the economies of all the Western nations were in the midst of the longest, deepest depression of all time. In fact, it was so long and so deep that it became known as 'The Great Depression'—as you probably know. The classical economics, which, as Keynes pointed out, dominated the thought of the 'governing and academic classes' of the times, held that such a thing was impossible. According to the classical economists, unemployment was a self-correcting problem. They viewed the labor market as being like any other market, and felt that unemployment, which they thought of as being a surplus of labor, would automatically be corrected by the interaction of supply and demand. That is, if there was unemployment then the price of labor—wages— would fall to the point where it would be profitable for employers to hire more people. Therefore, unemployment was theoretically impossible."

"Ah, I'm not sure I got that," I stammered, feeling ill.

"Look, if you were unemployed, wouldn't it be logical to expect you to go to the nearest factory and say 'I will work for you at a wage lower than your lowest-paid employee.' And isn't it just as logical to expect that they would hire you under those conditions?"

"Yes, I guess so."

"Therefore, there could never be unemployment. Wages would fall to the point where everyone was employed. Keynes's point was that this doesn't happen in the real world. Wages aren't flexible downward because of institutional constraints, unions, tradition, and the fact that once people get used to a certain wage they will resist taking a lower-paying job. So, Keynes argued that full employment was a special case. To run the

economy at full employment, if we can assume full employment to be a desirable state of affairs, requires conscious policy actions by the government. So, write this down:"

SINCE WAGES TEND NOT

TO BE FLEXIBLE DOWNWARD,

UNEMPLOYMENT IS THE GENERAL CASE.

I thought I was beginning to get the point. But, he went on.

"And there's more. If you are unemployed you are not producing anything. So, the economy is not operating at full capacity. But equally important is the fact that you are not buying anything either. So, when you have unemployment you have underconsumption, too. This was important in Keynes's time and it's even more important today as more and more jobs are being replaced by robots and computers. Here's an idea I don't think you're likely to forget: Robots can make an automobile, but they will never buy one," he said. "Write that down."

ROBOTS CAN MAKE

AN AUTOMOBILE, BUT

THEY WILL NEVER

BUY ONE.

He was right. That's something I'm not likely to forget.

"Now," he said, "let's think back to Mr. Keynes and his problem. He was living in a time of prolonged unemployment. All the economics he had been taught told him that unemployment was nothing more than a surplus in the labor market. So, unemployment, like any other surplus, should be a self-correcting problem. Competition for jobs among unemployed workers would reduce wages, and eventually full employment would be reestablished. Yet unemployment persisted. Economic theory and economic reality were in conflict. In effect, classical economics was posing a question to Keynes that Marx—Groucho Marx—also raised: 'Who are you gonna believe, me or your own eyes?' So, what Keynes did was develop a new theory, his *general theory*, to explain what determines the overall level of employment." ·

"And how does that work?" I asked.

"Well, think of the economy like a bathtub," he said. "You take baths on occasion, don't you?"

"Of course."

"Have you ever started to run your tub—gotten the water temperature just right—gone off to do something else, and come back later only to find that the tub was empty?"

"Yes, once or twice."

"What happened?"

"I'd forgotten to close the drain," I said, feeling a bit silly.

"Yes, go on."

"Well, the drain wasn't closed and the water ran out of it just as fast as it was coming in through the faucet."

"Exactly. If you start with an empty bathtub and run water into it just as fast as it runs out the drain, then you'll wind up with an empty bathtub. If you start with water in the tub and you run more in at the same rate as it leaks out the drain, the level of water will stay the same, right?"

"Yes. I've done that before. You know, when the water starts to get cold. I crack open the drain just a little bit to let some out, and then run some hot in . . ." I stammered to a halt, afraid to tell him more about my bathing habits than he wanted to know.

"That's wonderful," he said, with only a hint of sarcasm, "because you can think of our economy like a bathtub, which is partly filled with water. All your practical experience with this will be useful." Then he leaned back in his chair and sort of chuckled to himself.

"We're going to suppose that this bathtub has *two* faucets and *two* drains. The level of water in the tub represents the level of economic activity or the level of employment. When the tub is full of water, we'll call that full employment, or the full employment level of economic activity. If the U.S. economy were at full employment, that would be around a hundred twenty million jobs, give or take a few million.

"Now," he continued, "if water is coming in the two faucets at exactly the same rate that it is going out the two drains, the level of water in the bathtub will stay the same, correct?"

"Yes, sir, it would."

"Suppose you wanted more water in the tub. How could you get the level of water to rise?"

"Well, I suppose I could either open up the faucets so that water comes in faster or close the drains some so that it goes out slower, right?"

"That's right. Now, suppose you had more water in the tub than you wanted. How could you reduce the level of water?"

"By either closing the faucets some so that water comes in more slowly or opening up the drains so that it goes out faster."

"That's correct. And that's pretty much how government controls the economic system. Since government is able to influence various expenditure flows in the economy, it is also able to influence the overall level of economic activity, just like we are able to influence the level of water in our bathtubs by messing around with the faucets and the drains. Keynes argued that the overall level of economic activity is determined by the overall level of expenditures. Government is able to influence consumer expenditures and investment expenditures through its policies on taxes and interest rates and also by spending money itself. So, government is able to control the economy by influencing the overall level of consumer expenditures, investment expenditures, and government expenditures. Write that down."

GOVERNMENT CONTROLS THE ECONOMY

BY INFLUENCING THE OVERALL LEVEL

OF

CONSUMER EXPENDITURES,

INVESTMENT EXPENDITURES,

AND GOVERNMENT EXPENDITURES.

Having said that, he looked around on his desk for a moment. Then, rummaging through his wastebasket, he pulled out an envelope.

"Now imagine," he said, as he sketched a bathtub on the back of the envelope, "that some water is leaking out of one of the drains. Let's call that savings. What will happen?"

"The level of water in the bathtub will go down," I said, feeling a bit more sure of myself.

"Yes, of course. And, in the real world, what happens if savings leak out of the system? What happens if you take part of your salary and hide it under your mattress instead of spending it? Someone, somewhere, loses their job!" he said, answering his own question.

A Bathtub Approach
to
Macroeconomics

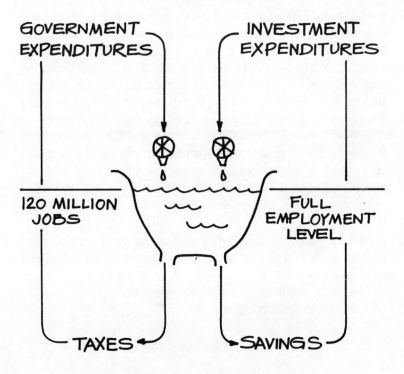

"But I don't hide my extra money under my mattress. I put it in the bank. Doesn't the bank lend it back out?" I said, vaguely remembering a course I had taken in money and banking a few years ago.

"Well, maybe they do and maybe they don't. They certainly would like to, but it all depends on whether anyone wants to borrow it. If someone does, and the money is invested—or injected back into the economy—then another job is created and the level of water in the bathtub will stay the same." He pointed to the investment faucet he had sketched on the envelope. "There's more than one source of jobs in our economy. If you work in a grocery store, you have a consumption-dependent job, which you might lose if people don't buy groceries. But if you work in construction, building new grocery stores, you have an investment-dependent job. You lose your investment-dependent job if someone doesn't feel it is going to be profitable to make the investment. Whether people will be willing to make investments depends on interest rates. In fact, almost everything depends on interest rates. High interest rates discourage investment while low interest rates encourage people to invest. Write that down."

INVESTMENT BEHAVIOR DEPENDS
ON INTEREST RATES.
IN FACT, ALMOST EVERYTHING
DEPENDS ON INTEREST RATES.
HIGH INTEREST RATES
DISCOURAGE INVESTMENT;
LOW INTEREST RATES
ENCOURAGE INVESTMENT.

I wrote it down, wondering why I had never quite understood it before. "So, that's why you always hear so much talk about investment," I said. "But I don't really understand what interest rates have to do with all this," I added, trying hard to remember back to my money and banking class.

"Well, like all of this, it is really pretty straightforward," he replied. "If you had a chance to buy a grocery store that would give you a return of twelve percent on your investment, would you do it?"

"Well, I don't know. It depends, I guess," I said, feeling a bit confused.

"Depends on what?"

"On the rate of interest I would have to pay to borrow the money?"

"Right! Now, suppose that interest rates are fourteen percent," he said, lighting his pipe again. "Would you buy the store?"

"No, I don't think so."

"Why?"

"Because I would be paying fourteen percent for the money and only earning twelve percent on the store. I'd be losing two percent on the deal." I felt like someone had switched on a light bulb in my head. Any idiot would know that, I thought.

"So, let's assume that banks lower interest rates to ten percent. Would you invest in the store then?"

"Sure," I responded. "Then I could make a two percent profit. So, if you want to increase investment, you lower interest rates. And the Federal Reserve Bank can do that. I remember that from my money and banking class," I said, feeling better because I had remembered something from school. "So, you can adjust the faucet to vary the amount of water coming in—in the form of investment—by changing interest rates."

"You've got it. The Federal Reserve Bank can influence investment by changing interest rates. Write that down."

THE FEDERAL RESERVE BANK
CAN INFLUENCE INVESTMENT
BY CHANGING INTEREST RATES.

"But you said the tub has two faucets and two drains. What about the other pair?" I asked, looking at the sketch he had drawn on the envelope.

"The other faucet represents government expenditures, and the other drain represents taxes. When the government takes part of your salary in taxes, water leaks out of the bathtub just like it does in the case of savings. And, the effect is the same. Someone loses a job unless the money is recycled back into the economy. This is done through government spending. There are actually three ways you can have a job in this economy. Consumption is one, investment is another, and government is the third. And, interestingly enough, about one-third of us work for government, if you count state and local governments along with the federal government. So, we can increase the level of the water, or the level of economic activity, by either increasing the rate at which the water flows into the tub—in the form of government expenditures—or decreasing the rate at which it flows out in the form of taxes."

Now I understood. "It works the other way around, too, doesn't it?" I asked.

"What do you mean?"

"Well, we can decrease the level of economic activity by decreasing the level of government expenditures, so that water flows in more slowly, or by increasing taxes so that it goes out faster."

"You've got it."

"O.K. Now, let me be sure I have this straight. We can increase the overall level of economic activity by increasing government expenditures or by decreasing taxes, and we can decrease the overall level of economic activity by decreasing government expenditures or increasing taxes."

"You've got it straight. Now, to make sure you remember it, why don't you write it down?"

TO INCREASE THE LEVEL

OF ECONOMIC ACTIVITY,

INCREASE GOVERNMENT EXPENDITURES

OR

DECREASE TAXES.

TO DECREASE THE LEVEL

OF ECONOMIC ACTIVITY,

DECREASE GOVERNMENT

EXPENDITURES

OR

INCREASE TAXES.

While I was writing, he got up from his desk, walked over to the couch, and put his feet up on the coffee table. "To keep the economy operating at a constant level of employment, or a constant level of economic activity, we have to keep government expenditures and investment equal to taxes and savings."

I was astonished. "Do you mean," I said, "that's all there is to it?"

"Well, like a lot of things in economics, it isn't quite that simple. Obviously we could have a situation where savings and taxes were equal to investment and government spending and still have unemployment. The level of water can be stable without the tub being full. Actually, that was Keynes's major point. There is no guarantee that the level of economic activity will automatically stabilize at full employment. It could stabilize at some point below full employment, in which case we would have unemployment and a recession or depression. Or, it could stabilize at some level above full employment—with the tub overflowing—and we'd have inflation. But, once the economy is stabilized at full employment, government expenditures and investment must equal taxes and savings. Any variation from this will cause either unemployment or inflation. Write that down."

ONCE THE ECONOMY IS AT

FULL EMPLOYMENT

WE MUST KEEP

SAVINGS AND TAXES EQUAL TO

GOVERNMENT EXPENDITURES

AND INVESTMENT.

ANY VARIATION FROM THIS

WILL CAUSE INFLATION OR

UNEMPLOYMENT.

"I think I'm beginning to understand," I said, "but how is this actually done, and, by the way, what does this have to do with me as a manager?"

"What it has to do with you as a manager is that if you are to be a successful planner—and that's what management is mostly about—you need to have some idea of what is going to happen to your organization when the government starts tinkering around with the economy. And the government is tinkering around with the economy all the time." Saying this, he refilled his pipe, studying it critically, the way pipe smokers do.

"The way it's actually done in the real world is what you read about on the front page of the newspaper every day. You've probably been reading it, but you obviously never really understood what it means. The reality is that the economy is controlled by the federal government and the Federal Reserve Bank—or the FED, as it is called—which is the central bank in the United States. The FED, by the way, operates independently of Congress and the president. So it makes its own policy, and its policy may or may not be consistent with what the government is doing. Anyway, the government has two tools and the FED has two. Taken together these are sometimes called the 'Keynesian toolkit,' although I doubt that Lord Keynes would approve of this if he were around today.

"Anytime it wants to, the government can increase or decrease the level of government spending. This either creates jobs or eliminates them. Or, it can decrease or increase taxes, which does the same thing. And the FED can either increase or decrease the money supply, which determines how much money banks have to lend out and hence the level of interest rates. Or, the FED can just increase or decrease interest rates directly by changing the interest rate it charges banks to borrow money. By the way, the interest rate the FED charges on loans is called the discount rate. You've heard of that, haven't you?"

"Yes, sir."

"The impact," he continued, "of changing the discount rate is more psychological than real, but that doesn't matter. The point is, it works. The FED is able to influence interest rates and therefore the level of investment. So, essentially, the economy is controlled by the federal government and the Federal Reserve Bank. This is done with fiscal policy, which involves adjusting the levels of government expenditures and taxation, and monetary policy, which involves controlling the supply of money and interest rates. The way these policy tools are used depends on the social and economic goals of the administration in power. Write that down."

ESSENTIALLY, THE ECONOMY IS

CONTROLLED BY

THE FEDERAL GOVERNMENT,

WITH FISCAL POLICY

—TAXES AND EXPENDITURES—

AND BY

THE FEDERAL RESERVE BANK,

WITH MONETARY POLICY

—THE MONEY SUPPLY

AND INTEREST RATES.

THE WAY THESE TOOLS ARE USED

DEPENDS ON THE GOALS OF

THE ADMINISTRATION IN POWER.

Writing frantically, I said, "This is getting complicated."

"It really isn't that difficult to understand," he said. But he looked at me skeptically, as if he were wondering whether I had what it takes to be a manager. "Just think about the Keynesian toolkit. Suppose we have a high rate of unemployment and you are the President's economic advisor. What would you tell the President to do?"

"Well, let's see," I said, wishing I had a pipe to fiddle with. "What I'd want to do is raise the level of water in the bathtub, right?"

"That's right."

"Well . . ., if we increased government spending, that would create some jobs. Or, we could cut taxes, and that would give everyone more money so they would spend more and that would create more jobs. Or, we could increase the money supply. That would give banks more money to lend so that interest rates would fall and investment would increase. Or, I guess we could just lower interest rates directly by reducing the discount rate. Or we could do all of those things."

"You've got it."

"But if we did all those things, wouldn't the bathtub overflow? I mean, wouldn't that cause inflation?"

As I said that, he smiled. He actually smiled for the first time that morning. In fact, I thought he was going to break out laughing. "That's the whole point," he said. "It's a question of trade-offs."

"Trade-offs between what?"

"Well, economics is all about trade-offs. In this case, the trade-off is between unemployment and inflation. Policies that are designed to reduce unemployment are likely to lead to inflation. If you want to slow down the rate of inflation, you can cut government spending, increase taxes, decrease the money supply, and increase interest rates. But that would slow down economic activity, eliminate jobs, and increase unemployment. Anything you do to reduce inflation will increase unemployment, and anything you do to reduce unemployment will, sooner or later, lead to increased inflation. The problem is one of trying to fine tune the economy. Macroeconomics explains how you can control the trade-off between inflation and unemployment. Write that down."

MACROECONOMICS EXPLAINS HOW YOU

CAN CONTROL THE TRADE-OFF

BETWEEN

UNEMPLOYMENT AND INFLATION.

"Now," he said, "let's go to lunch."

I was ready, to say the least. We walked across the quadrangle to the faculty club. It was a crisp fall day and there was a sense of football in the air. Some students—who looked young to me—were playing Frisbee on the lawn. Others were lying in the sun reading. I realized, to my surprise, that I was going to miss being back on campus that fall.

We sat down at a table in the corner. While it was obvious that everyone knew him, no one offered to join us. They must have thought I was a student.

"The usual, Professor Marshall?" the young waitress asked. She was obviously a student and very pretty.

"Yes, Becky, thanks. And what would you like, Bob?" he said, calling me by my first name for the first time.

"What would you recommend, sir?" I asked, wondering what "the usual" was.

"The Bison Burger," he said, matter-of-factly.

"I'll have the Bison Burger with coffee, please," I told Becky, trying hard to keep my mind on business. I was thinking I had better ask some intelligent questions soon, since he didn't seem like the type who would want to talk about football.

Then he said, "Did you see the Steelers' game last night?"

"No, sir," I replied. "I don't follow football very closely. Somehow it never interested me very much."

"If you are going to be a manager you had better get interested in it," he said, to my amazement.

"Why is that, sir?" I asked, beginning to feel like I had better change the subject.

"All managers like football," he replied, as if it were obvious. Now I knew it was time to change the subject.

"I must say, sir, that I enjoyed this morning very much. I learned more than I did in five semesters of economics. But there is one thing that bothers me."

"And that is . . .?" He took a sip of the martini Becky had just brought him. It was *at least* a double, and there were no fewer than four olives at the bottom of the glass. I wished I had ordered one. At least now I knew what "the usual" was.

I sipped my coffee and said, "From what you have said, it seems to me that controlling the economy, that is, keeping it running at full employment, should be a pretty simple job. If that's true, why are we having so many problems? Why do we have such persistently high unemployment, and high inflation?"

"Well," he said, "first of all, in economics it's not too hard to make almost anything look like it will work in theory; but the reality is often quite different. Adam Smith's perfectly competitive world looks very attractive in theory until you begin to realize that many of his assumptions don't, in reality, hold. His notion of competition, for example, doesn't make much sense in a world where the largest five hundred corporations control eighty percent of the economy. But actually, for quite a while it looked as if Keynesian theory had all the answers; during the twenty or so years following the war we were keeping the rates of unemployment and inflation within so-called 'normal' limits—about three or four percent each—on the average. That's when economics became the 'Queen of the Social Sciences' and even Nixon became a Keynesian . . ."

Our lunch arrived. A Bison Burger: "two all beef patties, special sauce, lettuce, cheese, pickles, onions on a sesame seed bun!" I thought to myself. But, it looked good enough.

He continued. "Around 1965, a number of things started happening that we were unable to predict, much less control. President Johnson wanted very much to expand our social welfare programs. That involved a lot more government spending. He also decided to get us involved in a war in Viet Nam. You understand what it means to increase government spending, don't you?"

"Yes, sir. It's inflationary unless you increase taxes at the same time," I replied, feeling more confident.

"That's right. But Johnson waited too long to raise taxes, and that was the beginning of an inflationary spiral that took us more than ten years to bring under control. Of course, there are other things. The OPEC countries, as you know, were able to increase the price of oil by about fifteen hundred percent between 1971 and 1981. Since the entire U.S. economy is built on the assumption of cheap oil supplies, that was an inflationary shock that we never adjusted to. Then there is international competition. When we helped Japan and Western Europe rebuild their economies after the war, we also helped them modernize all their plants and equipment, so that now they—especially Japan—may soon be more efficient and productive than we are. This put a lot of pressure on us to keep our inflation rate down so as not to price ourselves out of the export market, and, at the same time, had some very negative effects on our unemployment problem. International competition itself cost us a lot of jobs—some twenty-five percent of all the automobiles sold in the U.S. are now produced abroad, mostly in Japan. That translates into a lot of jobs. Another thing is that gearing monetary and fiscal policy to slow down the inflation rate is by definition—remember the trade-offs—going to raise the unemployment rate. You add to that the fact that the computer revolution and automation in general are replacing people faster than we can even think about training them for new jobs, and you have a very difficult and complicated situation. And I've only touched on the major points."

"Dessert, sir?" The waitress was back.

"Yes, please, Becky. The usual."

"And you, sir?"

"The same."

"The problem," he continued, "is with the exogenous variables—things that happen outside the economic system that we can't predict. As you saw this morning, we *do know* how to make the economy run at full employment. But we *don't know* how to predict what OPEC is going to do with oil prices, and, we can't predict the weather any better than the meteorologists."

"One other thing I have been wondering about, sir, is all this talk we hear about the deficit."

"Yes. What about it?"

"Well," I said, starting to feel uncomfortable again, "I can see now how deficits would occur when the government uses fiscal policy to stimulate the economy. Is that all there is to it? Is the reason we have such large deficits because the government has been trying to reduce unemployment?"

"That is certainly part of it. But it is by no means the

whole story. When Reagan took office in January of 1981 the U.S. economy was experiencing extraordinarily high rates of inflation and high rates of unemployment. Situations like that present policymakers with a nasty dilemma, as I'm sure you know."

"You mean in terms of the trade-off between unemployment and inflation?"

"Precisely. Anything you do to reduce unemployment is likely to make the inflation worse. On the other hand, if you try to reduce inflation, you're likely to wind up increasing unemployment. Reagan's strategy was to use monetary policy to fight inflation and to use fiscal policy to fight unemployment. In part this was by accident. In part, it was by design.

"Quite often the interests of the administration in power and the interests of the Federal Reserve Bank do not coincide. The politicians will always want the economy to be operating as closely as possible to full employment, especially at election time. But the FED will usually be more concerned about inflation than it is about unemployment. Most economists would agree that this is so because the FED represents the interests of the banking system. In fact, the FED is owned by the commercial banks. Bankers don't like inflation because they are creditors. High rates of inflation mean that loans are paid back with cheaper dollars; that is, inflation benefits debtors. Also, what really counts in the banking business is the *real rate of interest*, the difference between the interest rate and the inflation rate. For banks to make money, interest rates have to be higher than the inflation rate, historically about four percent higher . . ."

I was happy to see dessert arrive. Becky put a martini in front of each of us. I really appreciated "the usual" by this time. He lit his pipe and went on.

"Of course bankers don't really mind high interest

rates, since the interest rate is simply the price of the product they sell: money. But, obviously, there is a point where interest rates can get so high that they depress the demand for borrowing, and then everybody loses . . ."

"Everybody loses?" I asked.

"Yes, everybody. Banks lend less, consumers and investors borrow less, and everything grinds to a halt. That's what happened in 1980 and 1981, and that is mostly what pushed us into the recession of 1981– 1982. The Reagan administration had cut taxes and increased government spending—mostly defense spending—while the FED kept the money supply tight and interest rates high. It wasn't until the middle of 1982, when the FED began to loosen up and interest rates began to fall, that the economy started to grow again.

"So," he continued, "what we had was a situation of *contradictory* monetary and fiscal policy. And it was almost total chaos. We didn't begin to come out of the recession until the administration and the FED began to move in the same direction. And that's my point: For the Keynesian macroeconomic theory to work you have to have *consistent* monetary and fiscal policies. Otherwise, things can just go haywire."

"I'm still a bit confused," I said, "about what all this has to do with the deficit."

"To understand where we are with this now, you have to have a sense of how we got here, and that's what I'm trying to explain to you.

"During the 1980 campaign Reagan promised to cut taxes, increase defense expenditures, and reduce social welfare expenditures. And, as I said before, he wanted the FED to use restrictive monetary policies to reduce inflation.

"The FED's restrictive monetary policies tipped the

economy into a recession, which is part of the reason we have such high deficits. When the economy goes into a recession, tax revenues decrease because fewer people are working and paying income taxes, the incomes of those who are working are not rising as fast, and corporate profits, and hence corporate income tax payments, are lower. At the same time, government expenditures automatically increase because more people are collecting unemployment insurance and more people are on the welfare rolls than would otherwise be the case. So, part of the deficits we've seen over the past few years have been the result of the recession."

"But the economy is recovering now," I cut in. "Shouldn't the deficit automatically reduce itself?"

"And why should that happen?"

"Shouldn't tax revenues increase as more people are working and incomes and profits start to rise? And shouldn't expenditures decrease as fewer people are collecting unemployment insurance and welfare?"

"Yes. That's true. However, only a part of the deficits in recent years have been due to the recession. The rest is due to tax cuts that were not matched by cuts in expenditures. The result is that we'll still have very high deficits when the economic recovery is complete. This is what economists call 'structural deficits,' built-in deficits that will occur when the economy is operating at full employment."

"So," I said, "the problem is that the deficits we face in future years aren't going to go away by themselves. They're built into the budget." I thought I was beginning to understand it now.

"That's certainly the major reason why we are facing such large deficits, but that isn't what is really problematic about the deficits. The real problem is that the deficits will absorb a large part of the private savings that are expected to occur over the next few years. This

is money that would otherwise go for private investment in plant and equipment and housing. Ultimately,
that means slower economic growth and slower increases in everyone's standard of living.

"In the short run, deficits mean higher interest rates.
When the private economy is growing and the government goes into capital markets to finance the deficit,
that has the effect of driving up the interest rates. Higher
interest rates lead to a number of problems. We get an
'unbalanced recovery,' because interest-sensitive sectors of the economy, like the housing and automobile
industries, won't keep pace with other sectors. High
interest rates also help keep the value of the dollar high,
which reduces the competitiveness of U.S. goods in international markets. High interest rates in the U.S. also
lead to higher interest rates worldwide, which may or
may not be consistent with the macroeconomic policy
goals of Western European countries and Japan, and
which definitely make for tough sledding for Third World
countries who are trying to roll over their debts."

"But couldn't the FED use its monetary policy tools
to keep interest rates down?" I asked.

"They could, but then you run the risk of overheating
the economy and starting a new round of inflation."

"And if they hold the line on interest rates . . ."

"Then they run the risk of tipping the economy into
another recession, because we'd have another case of
contradictory monetary and fiscal policies and things
going haywire again, just like they did back in the early
1980s.

"So, you can perhaps see by now that all this is very
complicated. If it were just a question of manipulating
the Keynesian model, applying the tools, then economists wouldn't have much to do. But politics can never
be separated from economic policy, and there are always random events—random shocks, we call them—

which we can never anticipate. That's why you hear so many jokes these days about economists not knowing what they are doing. You've heard those, haven't you?"

"I'm not sure," I replied.

"Well, one of the old favorites is 'if you laid all the economists in the world end to end, they could never reach a conclusion.' "

I *had* heard that one, but I pretended to laugh.

"Another is that 'economists are the only professional group in the world that would get into a circle if you asked them to form a firing squad.' "

This time, I didn't have to pretend.

"In physics, as a famous economist once noted, you don't have to worry about the speed of light changing every day; you can *assume* it will stay constant. In economics we have to make assumptions. However, the only assumption we can really depend on is that things are going to change. Human behavior is not a constant.

"There is one last point," he continued, "and then we have to go to class."

I didn't know we were "going to class," but I certainly wasn't going to say anything. Instead, I finished my martini. And so did he. Becky brought coffee for both of us, and cleared the table. We were the only ones left in the dining room.

"In the long run, high interest rates also lead to higher deficits. With a two hundred billion-dollar deficit, each additional percentage point increase in the interest rate adds two billion dollars to the government's interest costs for financing the current deficit and to much higher total interest costs for financing the national debt, which is on its way toward two trillion dollars now."

"You know, sir, that is one point I have never really understood. What is the difference between the debt and the deficit?"

"Well, the deficit is simply the difference between what the government takes in and what it spends in any given year. The national debt, on the other hand, is the accumulation of all the deficits in previous years that we haven't paid off."

"So, the deficits that we have been running in the past have simply added to the national debt."

"That's right."

"And when we hear that the deficit for 1983 was something like a hundred and ninety-five billion dollars, that means that the government spent a hundred and ninety-five billion dollars *more* than it took in in that year alone."

"You've got it."

"And that hundred and ninety-five billion dollars was also added to the national debt."

"Correct." Professor Marshall signed the bill and then said "Let's go to class" in such a way that I knew I didn't have much choice. It was almost one-thirty.

As we walked across the quad, he explained, "Today is the first day of class, and I'm meeting my graduate seminar in Managerial Economics. I think you can see by now why it is important for a manager to understand something about how the economy functions. But, in your day-to-day work as a manager, what you really need to understand is the theory of how business firms operate. That's why I'm taking you to this class. Don't take notes unless I write something on the blackboard. When I do, write it down."

2

What Every Manager Needs to Know about Microeconomics

W e walked into the classroom and there, to my surprise, sat Becky. There were several other students in the room, too. The walls were pale green. Two panels of blackboard stretched across the front of the room and a third ran along one of the side walls. There were three tiers of long, semicircular tables with eight or ten soft, swivel chairs behind each one. The professor walked to the front of the room, placed his briefcase on the right side of a table, got a short lectern from the corner, and put it on the left side of the table. Someone had chalked: "IT'S BEEN LONELY IN MY SADDLE SINCE MY HORSE DIED" on the front of the lectern.

Soon everyone was laughing. They had not yet quieted down by the time the professor finished arranging his notes, but he smiled, and it was obvious he knew it was there.

"Good afternoon," he said, in a rather loud voice. The class quieted immediately. "I am Professor Marshall and this is 51–640, the graduate seminar in Managerial Economics. I'm going to pass around this piece of paper, which is something called a class roster. If your name is not on it, I suggest you report to window D in the registrar's office—it will be the one with a long line. I don't require regular attendance in this course. The only reason to come is if you want a passing grade."

The professor continued. "What I would like to do

today is discuss the commonsense reasoning that lies behind the major economic concepts we will be investigating in this course. Most of the rest of the course will be taken up with developing a mathematical elaboration of these concepts and of their applications. The math is sort of a barrier that we in the economics profession have erected to confuse the layman, reduce the number of people who can call themselves economists, and keep our salaries high . . ."

Becky laughed at this, and so did several other students. The entire class visibly relaxed.

"Don't misunderstand me. The mathematics of economics is important, and if you don't know it, you won't pass this course. At the same time, there is a very real danger that, in trying to understand the math, you'll lose sight of what it all really means."

"Amen to that!" I thought to myself.

"Let me begin by asking a question. What is it that a manager really needs to know about economics?"

A very intense young man in freshly pressed jeans and a yellow oxford cloth shirt volunteered, "How to make money?"

"How to handle business finances?" asked an attractive woman with long red hair.

"How to run the business efficiently?" This question came from a bearded young man in the back row.

The professor shook his head from side to side rather sorrowfully. Then looked around the room to see if there were other ideas. There weren't. "Perhaps I should rephrase the question," he said. "What is it that businesses are in business to do?"

"Well," said the bearded young man, "there are all sorts of different businesses. I mean, it isn't possible to generalize about something like that, is it?"

The fellow in the yellow shirt said, "Well, they all produce some sort of good or service or try to sell something, or . . ."

"Profits." It was Becky. "Businesses exist to make profits."

"That's right! Profits are what it's all about. The goal of business is to make profits, and your job as managers is to make profits for the firm. And it isn't simply a matter of trying to make *some* profits. The goal is to *maximize* profits." Then he turned to the board and wrote:

PROFITS

EQUAL

TOTAL REVENUES

MINUS

TOTAL COSTS.

"Almost all of what we'll be doing in this course will be concerned with investigating this concept.

"Let's think about it for a minute in the simplest possible form. Suppose you're going to introduce a new product, a solar-powered, variable-speed, electric tooth-brush, or something along those lines. How many would you want to produce, and what price would you charge for them?"

No one answered.

"Obviously, there is no way to answer that question without more information. The first thing you would want to do is to conduct a market survey to find out something about the demand for your new product. You've probably already learned how to do one in your marketing courses. If you haven't, you soon will.

"Now, suppose you've done your survey, analyzed all the data, and decided to sell the product for twenty-five dollars apiece. Let's further suppose that you are selling one thousand units a month at that price. What would your total revenue be?"

"Twenty-five thousand per month!" said the bearded fellow.

"Good. Now, let's suppose that it costs you eighteen dollars apiece to manufacture your product. What would your total cost be?"

"Eighteen thousand per month," said the redheaded woman.

"Fine, so what would your profits be?"

"Seven thousand per month," said the fellow in the yellow shirt.

"That's right. Now, the question is, is that the best you can do? Is that the most profit you can make?"

This time, there was no reply.

"Clearly, to answer that question, you need to have more information. In particular, you'd have to have some idea of how your revenues and costs would behave as you charged different prices, and produced and sold different amounts of your product, right?"

Everyone seemed to agree with this.

"Now, we want to work with as simple an example as possible. So, let's suppose that costs of production are not important. And let's imagine that we have an inexhaustible supply of free, solar-powered, variable-speed, electric toothbrushes. In situations like this, where your costs don't vary as the amount of the product you sell changes, the way to maximize profits is to maximize total revenues." To underscore the point, he went to the board and wrote:

IF COSTS DON'T CHANGE

AS OUTPUT CHANGES, THEN

TO MAXIMIZE PROFITS

SIMPLY MAXIMIZE TOTAL REVENUE.

"How can you do that?" asked the young man in the yellow shirt.

"Good question. How could you?"

"You could lower your price and see if you could sell more units of the product," suggested the bearded fellow.

Picking up on the general drift of the discussion, the young man in yellow asked, "How about raising prices?"

"Well, let's see," said the professor. "Suppose you lowered your price to twenty-two fifty, and that your sales increased to eleven hundred units per week. Then what would your total revenues be?"

As everyone scrambled around to get out their pocket calculators, Becky said, "Your revenues would fall to twenty-four thousand, seven hundred and fifty dollars."

"So that was obviously not a good plan was it?"

Everyone seemed to agree that it wasn't.

"You see," he said, "if you're going to monkey around with prices in order to try and increase your revenues, you have to know something about the demand for your product. That is, you have to know something about how changes in price will influence the sales of your product. In other words, you have to know something about the price elasticity of demand for your product."

He took two large rubber bands out of his pocket, a red one which was quite thin and a very thick brown one, and handed them to the young man in the yellow shirt. "Think of these as two different products," he said. "Which is the most elastic?"

The young man stretched each in turn, and it was soon obvious to everyone that the red rubber band was quite elastic and that the brown one would hardly stretch at all. "The red one," he replied.

"Good," the professor said. "That's right.

"Now," he continued, "the basic concept of elasticity is quite simple. The question is: How responsive is the quantity demanded of a product to changes in its price?

From your point of view as a manager, knowing about the elasticity of demand for your product is important, because it tells you how changes in price can be expected to influence total revenues. If demand is very responsive to changes in price, then we'd say it is price elastic." He turned to the blackboard and wrote:

PRICE ELASTIC DEMAND:

PERCENTAGE CHANGE IN QUANTITY DEMANDED

IS GREATER THAN

PERCENTAGE CHANGE IN PRICE.

"When demand is elastic, a small percentage change in price will lead to a relatively larger percentage change in quantity demanded. So, when price is decreased, quantity demanded increases by a relatively larger amount, and total revenues will increase. For example, if you decreased price by five percent and quantity demanded increased by ten percent, then we'd say demand is elastic. With a five percent drop in price and a ten percent increase in unit sales, your total revenues would increase by five percent.

"On the other hand, if you increased price by five percent and your unit sales decreased by ten percent, demand would still be elastic. But your total revenues would fall, in this case by five percent. So, if the demand for your product is price elastic, the way to increase total revenues is to decrease price.

"The other possibility is that the demand for your product is price *in*elastic, just like our brown rubber band." Then he went to the board and wrote:

Price inelastic demand:

PERCENTAGE CHANGE IN QUANTITY DEMANDED

IS LESS THAN

PERCENTAGE CHANGE IN PRICE.

"When demand is inelastic, it doesn't respond much to changes in price. So, if demand is *inelastic*, the way to increase revenues is to *increase* price. Any given percentage increase in price will result in a smaller percentage decrease in quantity demanded, or unit sales. For example, you could increase price by fifteen percent, and unit sales would decrease by a smaller amount, say, eight percent. This is clearly a case where demand is price inelastic, and revenues have clearly increased, in this case by seven percent. On the other hand, if demand is inelastic and you decrease price, your total revenues will decrease, because the percentage decrease in price will be greater than the percentage increase in unit sales.

"The point here is that you have to know about the price elasticity of demand for your product if you're going to make good pricing decisions. Let me tell you a little story. About two years ago I met a man who was the manager of a particular product line for a local company. I was at the point in this course where we talk about the pricing behavior of firms, and so I was thinking about the issue a lot. When I got the chance, I asked him how he made his pricing decisions. He told me that he just estimated how many units he was going to sell, and then figured out how much revenue that would produce at the current price. If that was enough revenue, he didn't bother with a price change. If not, then, as he put it, 'You just jack up your price.' " The professor shook his head ruefully, and then continued, "The last time I ran into him, he was looking for a new job."

He paused for a moment, and laughter slowly spread throughout the class. However, the young man in the yellow shirt looked perplexed. "I don't get it," he said. "Why was he looking for a new job?"

The volume of laughter increased, much to the young man's dismay.

The professor appeared to give this question very careful thought. Then he said, "Well, one possibility is that my manager friend had somehow misjudged the elasticity of demand for his product. You see, higher prices will generate more revenue only if demand is inelastic."

"But," the young man in yellow persisted, "how can you tell whether the demand for your product is elastic or inelastic?"

"Now that," said the professor, "is a good question." This had the effect of quieting the class. "And that is one area where economists and market research people work very closely together. Although not, perhaps, as closely as they might, if my friend's sad story is any guide. Nonetheless, economists and market researchers can estimate how changes in price or changes in other attributes can be expected to influence the sales of a particular product. The branch of economics that does this kind of work is known as econometrics, and modern econometricians have an impressive array of statistical tools to use on precisely this sort of problem.

"In addition to these high-powered quantitative techniques, there are some basic principles of economics that we can use to investigate questions about elasticities. The two factors that play the most important role in determining whether the demand for a good is elastic or inelastic are the percentage of a consumer's income spent on it and the number of substitutes which are available for it. Let's take up each of these in turn.

"The larger the percentage of a consumer's income that is spent on something, the more elastic the demand for it is likely to be. So, we'd expect the demand for big ticket items like cars, houses, and personal computers to be fairly elastic. On the other hand, things that a relatively small percentage of income is spent on—salt, pepper, shoestrings, and the like—are in fairly inelastic demand. Can you see the reasoning behind that?"

The redheaded woman was quick to respond. "I think so," she said. "Is it the idea that consumers will tolerate price changes in things they don't spend much money on because their expenditures on those things simply don't amount to much?"

"Precisely.

"Now," he went on, "the other important influence on elasticity is the number of substitutes that are available. The more substitutes there are, the more elastic the demand is likely to be. Would someone care to tackle an explanation of that point?"

The young man in the yellow shirt was the first to speak. "If there are a lot of substitutes for a good, then consumers could just switch to something else. But, if there are only a few substitutes, then their options are more limited."

"That's right. Now, how about a couple of examples."

"Well," the same student continued, "gasoline would be an example of a good with few substitutes. So, I'd expect the demand for it to be pretty inelastic."

"And you'd be right."

"And . . ., well, the market for pocket calculators is a case in which demand would be elastic. There are a lot of different firms that make them. So, if the price of TI calculators goes up, people could always buy a Sharp or a Casio or some other brand, right?"

"That's right." Then he went to the board and, underneath the definition of elastic demand, wrote:

IF IT LOOMS LARGE IN THE BUDGET

OR HAS LOTS OF SUBSTITUTES,

ITS DEMAND IS PROBABLY ELASTIC;

DECREASE PRICE TO INCREASE REVENUES.

"That," he pointed out, "is a fair summary of what we've said about the case in which demand is elastic." Then he moved over to the other panel of the board, and, under the definition of inelastic demand, wrote:

IF IT DOESN'T COST MUCH

OR HAS VERY FEW SUBSTITUTES,

ITS DEMAND IS PROBABLY INELASTIC;

INCREASE PRICE TO INCREASE REVENUES.

"And that is a fair summary of what we have said about inelastic demand. The problem with trying to apply these principles is that we often run into cases where the two indicators point in different directions: things that cost a lot, but have few substitutes, or things which don't cost much, but have lots of substitutes. Then our general principles fail us, and the only solution is to get an economist to try to estimate the elasticity for us.

"Questions about any of that?"

For a moment, it looked like the bearded fellow in the back was going to raise a question. But he didn't.

"A third factor that plays an important role in determining elasticities is time. We'd expect the demand for any given product to be more elastic in the long run than in the short run. In part, this is because it takes consumers a while to respond to price changes. That is, it takes them a while to recognize that the price of a particular product has gone up and to adjust their consumption patterns accordingly. In part, it is due to the fact that many of the products consumers buy are complements of other goods that they already own, and they have to switch to other types of goods to reduce their consumption.

In the short run, consumers can respond to increases in gasoline prices by changing their driving habits. But over time, they can purchase more fuel-efficient cars. When the price of home heating oil began to rise, people could reduce their consumption of it by 'dialing down' their thermostats, weatherstripping doors and windows, and adding insulation. Over time, they can replace their oil-burning furnaces with gas furnaces or wood stoves or solar heating. But these adjustments take time. So, the upshot is that we'd expect the elasticities to increase over time."

"So, you're saying that we'd expect the demand for a product to be more responsive to changes in price over long periods of time than we would over short time periods?" asked the young man in the yellow shirt.

"You've got it."

The redheaded woman asked, "Is that all there is to making profits? I mean, is it simply a matter of finding a price to charge that will maximize revenues?"

"Well, that's all there is to it in cases where costs are not important, and there are some cases where they aren't. For example, if you're the manager of the local movie theatre, the biggest costs you face are for film rentals, and they're fixed by your contracts with distributors. So, the goal becomes one of setting ticket prices so that your revenues are maximized.

"On the other hand, there are a lot of situations where costs are an important consideration in the quest for maximum profits. In those cases, maximizing profits means picking the level of output where the difference between costs and revenues is the greatest." To underscore the point, he went to the board and wrote:

WHEN COSTS VARY WITH OUTPUT,

MAXIMIZING PROFITS

MEANS FINDING THE OUTPUT LEVEL

WHERE THE DIFFERENCE BETWEEN

TOTAL REVENUE AND TOTAL COST

IS GREATEST.

"Now," he continued, "one important cost concept economists use is the distinction between fixed and variable costs. Fixed costs are the costs that don't vary as output changes: the rent on buildings and machinery, interest payments on loans, insurance, and so forth. They're the costs that you have to pay even on Sunday, when you're closed down, and they're called fixed costs because they don't change as output changes. They're fixed. Get it?

"But variable costs do change as output changes, and the elements of variable costs are things like wages for hourly employees, materials costs, utilities bills, and so forth.

"We make the distinction because variable costs are the *only* costs that you need to take into account when making decisions about what level of output to produce. Fixed costs aren't important in these kinds of decisions because there's nothing you can do about them. By definition, they're costs that don't change as output changes. They are," and he paused for effect, "fixed.

"For example, there was a story in the paper the other day headlined 'Driving Costs are Twenty-Three and a Half Cents Per Mile' that reported the results of an annual study done by the American Automobile Association. What they do is take a new, mid-sized car and figure out all the costs of operating it for a year: insurance, license, registration, taxes, depreciation, finance charges, maintenance, gasoline, oil, and tires, based on the assumption that you drive fifteen thousand miles per year. This year, it worked out to be something like thirty-five hundred and twenty-five dollars. Then they divided that by fifteen thousand and came up with the twenty-three and a half cents per mile figure.

"The question is, is that right? Does it really cost twenty-three and a half cents per mile to drive your car?"

"Well, it all depends," said the young man in the yellow shirt. "If you had an older car . . ."

And that was as far as he got. "Let's stick with the example we have before us," said the professor. "The point I want to make here is that it is a mistake to lump fixed costs and variable costs together when you're making decisions. That's precisely what they've done in this story in the paper. Some of the costs they've included, like insurance, license, registration, taxes, and finance charges, are fixed. They don't vary with the amount of driving you do. They're the costs of *owning* a car. The variable costs in this case are the costs of gas, oil, and tires. It's these variable costs that are the costs of *driving* your car."

"Oh," said the young man in yellow, "I see."

"Now, let me show you how mixing the two together can lead you to make the wrong decision. Suppose you wanted to go to Springfield, which is about a hundred and thirty miles from here, and back. If you believe what you read in the paper, what would that cost?"

The young man in yellow's fingers flew over the keys of his calculator. "Sixty-one dollars and ten cents," said Becky.

"And suppose you could get a round trip bus ticket to Springfield for thirty dollars. What would you do?"

"Take the bus," said the young man. "I could save, uh . . . thirty-one dollars and ten cents that way."

"Could you? Let's think about it a minute. The twenty-three and a half cents per mile figure includes *all* the costs of the car. The important costs here are the variable costs, the costs of *driving* the car. And those work out to about eight cents per mile, or to about twenty-one dollars for driving to Springfield and back. You have to pay all the costs of *having* the car—the fixed costs—whether you drive it or leave it in the garage. And that's why people who have cars drive them and people who don't have cars ride the bus!" Then he went to the board and wrote:

VARIABLE COSTS

ARE THE COSTS TO CONSIDER

IN MAKING DECISIONS

ABOUT WHAT LEVEL OF OUTPUT

TO PRODUCE.

"The distinction between fixed and variable costs also helps us understand why it sometimes makes sense for firms to operate at a loss."

"But how," asked the bearded fellow, "would it ever make sense for a firm to operate at a loss? If you're losing money, shouldn't you just pack it in?"

"That depends. In some cases, the sensible thing to do is to shut down. However, in other cases, it does make sense to continue producing and just take your lumps. It depends on which approach will lead to the lowest losses. If the firm simply shuts down, it will have no revenues, but it will still have to cover its fixed costs. So, its losses would be exactly equal to its fixed costs. If it can produce and cover all of its variable costs, and at least some of its fixed costs, then it makes sense for the firm to operate at a loss. If you think about it, you can probably recall hearing about many cases of firms operating with losses. A few years ago, all the major automobile companies were losing money. The airlines have been having a tough time of it lately, too.

"Of course, over time, as firms continue to take losses, if there is no relief in sight, some of them will probably leave the industry. But, in the short run, as long as you can cover all your variable costs and some of your fixed costs, it makes sense to produce and take a loss.

"Now, there are two other important cost concepts that we need to understand: average cost and marginal cost." Then he went to the board and wrote:

AVERAGE COST

IS TOTAL COST

DIVIDED BY TOTAL OUTPUT.

■

MARGINAL COST

IS THE *CHANGE* IN

TOTAL COST

DUE TO A

CHANGE IN OUTPUT.

"Average cost, as economists use the term, is what people have in mind when they talk about cost per unit. Marginal cost is the cost of producing an *additional* unit. The difference between the two, and the relationship between them, is easy enough to understand if you think about it in terms of your grade point average. You all came into this class with some grade point average, a high one, I presume. Suppose it is a 'B' and you get an 'A' in this course, as unlikely as that might be. What happens to your average? It goes up, obviously. On the other hand, if you get a 'C' your average will go down. So, if you think about this class as your 'marginal course'—the extra being added to your total—it's clear that a higher marginal grade will raise your average and that a lower marginal grade will lower it. So, if average costs are going down, it's because marginal costs are lower than average costs. If average costs are going up, it's because marginal costs are higher than average costs.

"Marginal cost," he said pontifically, "is the queen of the cost concepts."

"Then which one is the king?" It was the bearded fellow.

"The king," he said flatly, "is dead."

"What does that mean?" I asked Becky.

"Elvis," she whispered.

"The other side of the profit equation has to do with revenues. The revenues of the firm depend on the price of its product and the number of units it sells. So, any discussion of revenues necessarily involves a discussion of the demand curve the firm faces. The demand curve for a product shows the relationship between the price of the product and the number of units of the product the firm can sell.

"In broad, general terms, economists identify two different demand situations that a firm might face. One is known as a perfectly competitive market. In a perfectly competitive market situation, the industry is composed of a large number of small firms, a large number of independent buyers, and each firm produces an identical product. Since each firm is small relative to the size of the market, no single firm can influence the price of the product by increasing or decreasing the amount it produces. Since there are a large number of buyers, no single buyer can influence price either. And, since all firms have products that are identical, one firm can't charge a price for its product that is any different from the price charged by its competitors. So, perfectly competitive markets are characterized by what is called 'price-taking behavior.' That is, individual buyers and sellers behave as if they have no influence over price."

"This," said the bearded fellow, "just doesn't seem very realistic to me. I mean, aren't most markets dominated by a few large firms that produce products that are at least a little bit different from their competitors' products?"

"Well," said the professor, "that's a good point, and I'd like to respond to it in a couple of ways. First, there *are* some real world markets that correspond pretty closely to the model of perfect competition. Markets for agricultural products like fruits, vegetables, grains, milk, and livestock are cases in point. And, there are other markets, the stock market and the market for bonds, for example, which operate a lot like a competitive market. Second, I did indicate that we'll be examining other types of market structures. Third, the model of perfect competition is attractive from a pedagogical point of view, because it's easy to understand. So, both because there are cases where the model can help us understand how markets work and because it's an easy place to begin, we'll want to spend some time looking at how a perfectly competitive market would work."

"I'm not sure," said the young man in the yellow shirt, "what you mean by price-taking behavior."

"Well, think about it for a minute. Most of us behave like price takers most of the time, don't we? Did you bargain over the price of anything the last time you went to the grocery store? Did you cut a deal on your lunch today?"

"Well, no. I didn't."

"That's price-taking behavior. Now, are there more questions about that?"

There weren't.

"O.K. Since each firm is so small relative to the size of the total market, it follows that it can sell as much or as little as it wants at the prevailing price. When Farmer Jones takes his wheat to market, he won't be bringing enough to cause the bottom to fall out of the market. If Farmer Smith's corn crop fails, that, by itself, won't cause corn prices to skyrocket. I can sell all my IBM stock and use the proceeds to buy GM stock and that won't cause the price of IBM stock to fall or the price of GM stock to rise.

"So, in a competitive situation, the firm's total revenues can be computed by simply multiplying the prevailing market price of the product by the number of units of the product the firm sells. And the firm's marginal revenue, which is the addition to total revenue that occurs due to selling an additional unit, will be equal to the price of the product. For example, suppose we're a wheat farmer and wheat is selling for four dollars a bushel. Our total revenue will be four hundred dollars if we sell a hundred bushels and four hundred and four dollars if we sell a hundred and one bushels. So, the addition to our revenues that resulted from our selling an additional bushel—that is, our marginal revenue—is four dollars, which is also the price of the product.

"That means the firm can always increase its revenues by increasing the amount of the product it sells. The catch is that, as the firm increases its output, it also increases its costs. So, as we have seen, the problem of profit maximization is a problem of choosing the output level where the difference between revenues and costs is the greatest.

"Now, marginal cost tells us what is happening to total costs as we increase output, and marginal revenue tells us what is happening to total revenue as we increase output. In fact, marginal cost is the rate at which total cost is changing, and marginal revenue is the rate at which total revenue is changing. Those of you who have had calculus will recognize that the marginal cost curve is the first derivative of the total cost curve and that marginal revenue is the first derivative of the total revenue curve.

"The profit maximizing rule is that we should produce that output where marginal revenue is equal to marginal cost." Then, to emphasize the point, he went to the blackboard and wrote:

TO MAXIMIZE PROFITS,

PRODUCE WHERE

MARGINAL REVENUE

EQUALS

MARGINAL COST.

"That," he said, "is our profit maximizing rule. I want to back into an explanation of it by showing that if marginal revenue isn't equal to marginal cost, the firm could increase or decrease its output and make a higher profit.

"If marginal revenue is greater than marginal cost, the firm can always increase its profits by increasing its output. For example, if the firm is producing some level of output where marginal revenue is two dollars and marginal cost is a dollar-fifty, the firm clearly stands to gain by increasing its output. Producing an additional unit will add two dollars to revenues and only a dollar-fifty to costs, so profits would increase by fifty cents if the firm produced that additional unit. But, as the firm increases its output, marginal costs increase, and it should continue to increase output up to the point where marginal revenue is exactly equal to marginal cost. At that point, the last unit produced would add two dollars to revenues and two dollars to costs, and total profits would be as large as possible.

"On the other hand, if marginal cost is greater than

marginal revenue, the firm could increase its profits by reducing its output. Suppose that we're producing some level of output where marginal cost is two dollars and fifty cents and marginal revenue is two dollars. That means that we've just sold something for two dollars that cost us two dollars and fifty cents to make. Not smart. So, what should we do?"

"Reduce output," said Becky.

"And what will happen?"

"Well," said Becky, "by reducing output by one unit, we'd reduce our revenues by two dollars and reduce our costs by two-fifty. So, we'd be fifty cents ahead of the game."

"I'm sorry, sir, but I'm afraid I just don't get it," said the young man in the yellow shirt.

"Let's suppose," said the professor, "that you're walking down the street and someone comes up to you and says, 'Excuse me, but do you have change for a five dollar bill?' and that you say, 'No, I'm sorry, all I have is three dollars' and they say, 'That's okay, I'll take it.' Would you do it?"

"Would I trade someone three dollars for five dollars?"

"That's the question."

"Of course."

"In that transaction, your marginal cost is three dollars and your marginal revenue is five dollars, and you'd have to say that making that trade was a good deal, wouldn't you?"

"Yes."

"That's the position you're in if you're producing some level of output where marginal revenue is greater than marginal cost. If you find yourself in that position, the thing to do is to increase output. The catch is that sooner or later marginal cost will start to rise. Eventually, marginal cost will rise to the point where it is equal to marginal revenue, and that is the output you want to produce in order to maximize profits. As I said before, as long as marginal revenue exceeds marginal cost, you can always increase your profits by increasing output. Do you see it now?"

"Yes."

"All right. Let's look at the other side of it. Suppose that you're the one who wants change for the five dollar bill. If the first person you walked up to said, 'No, I'm sorry, all I have is three dollars,' would you take it?"

"Well . . ., no, I wouldn't."

"Why not?"

"Well, in that case my marginal cost would be five dollars and my marginal revenue would only be three dollars."

"That's right, and if you find yourself producing some level of output where marginal cost is greater than marginal revenue, the thing to do is reduce output. As you do that, marginal cost will decline. Sooner or later it will fall to the point where it is equal to marginal revenue, and that's the level of output you should produce. Do you see it now?"

"Yes."

"Given that you have the option, it doesn't make sense to produce anywhere but at the point where marginal revenue equals marginal cost. Any other level of output will involve lower profits."

"Yes, sir," said the man. "I see that now. Thank you."

"Once you get the hang of it, marginal reasoning is a very powerful tool. And, you can apply it to all sorts of situations. For example, suppose you were mounting an advertising campaign and you had to figure out how to allocate your expenditures among radio, TV, and the newspapers. What you should do is divide your budget up so that the last dollar you spend on each type of advertising adds the same amount to your sales. That is, you should equate the marginal cost of each type of ad to the marginal revenue that it generates and the marginal costs and revenues of each to that of the others." Then he wrote:

IT MAKES ECONOMIC SENSE

TO PURSUE ANY ACTIVITY

UP TO THE POINT WHERE

THE MARGINAL BENEFIT OF IT

EQUALS

ITS MARGINAL COST.

"If the marginal, or additional, revenue you get from radio advertising is greater than the marginal cost of it, then you can increase your profits by increasing your expenditures on radio. And, if an additional dollar spent on newspaper ads will increase revenues more than an additional dollar spent on TV, then you should spend it on a newspaper ad. The notion that you should equate things at the margin like this lies at the very heart of microeconomic reasoning. That's why I said earlier that marginal cost is the queen of the cost concepts. For the same reason, marginal revenue is the queen of the revenue concepts.

"Now, let's get back to the model of perfect competition. Since marginal revenue is equal to price in a perfectly competitive market, that means that price will be equal to marginal cost. In fact, economists say that 'perfect competition is characterized by marginal cost pricing.'

"But for us to say anything more about profits, we have to look at the relationship between price and average cost. If price is greater than average cost, that means the firm is making a profit, and the firm's profit per unit will be equal to the difference between price and average cost.

"Of course it's possible for price to be below the lowest possible point on the firm's average cost curve. In that case, there is no level of output the firm can produce that will allow them to make a profit, and the firm's desire to maximize profits is translated into the desire to minimize losses. And, as we've already seen, so long as the firm can produce and cover all of its variable costs and at least some of its fixed costs, it will make sense for them to produce and take losses.

"Over time, if firms continue to take losses, they'll leave the industry. As they do this, the supply of the product will decrease, and the price will rise. Firms will continue to leave until price rises to the point where it is at least equal to average cost, and the remaining firms in the industry are breaking even.

"On the other hand, price might be high enough that existing firms in the industry are making profits. In this case, the profits being earned by existing firms will attract new firms into the industry. But, as new firms enter, supplies of the product increase and price begins to fall.

"So, the long-run tendency in a competitive market is for price to equal average cost, and for profits to equal zero."

"Now," said the redheaded woman, "let me make sure I have this straight. If price is greater than average cost, existing firms will be making a profit, right?"

"Yes."

"And that will cause new firms to want to enter the industry, which will cause price to fall, so that profits eventually disappear."

"Correct."

"So," she continued, "the whole quest for profits is really self-defeating?"

"Well, yes and no. In the short run, it is possible for new firms to enter the industry and share in the profits. But over the long haul, the profits do disappear. When you look at it in those terms it is sort of ironic, isn't it? But this is how the wonderful competitive world of Adam Smith is supposed to operate. The desire of firms to make profits leads them to develop new products and new production techniques, but, ultimately, competition from other producers forces prices down to the point where profits disappear."

"But why," asked the young man in the yellow shirt, "would a firm stay in business when it isn't making any profits?"

The professor thought about this for a moment, then said, "Well, this gets us into some material that I hadn't planned to discuss today, but since it's come up, we might as well work our way through it.

"The short version of the story is that economists have a somewhat different notion of profits than accountants. The difference is traceable to the way we think about costs. Economists distinguish between explicit costs and implicit costs.

"Explicit costs are out-of-pocket expenses. They represent actual cash outlays, and they are the only kind of costs that accountants look at.

"Implicit costs, or opportunity costs, are costs that you incur when you take one course of action as opposed to another. It's this notion of opportunity costs that leads economists to say, 'There is no such thing as a free lunch.'

"One way to get a handle on the distinction is to think your way through the following question: Why, since it doesn't cost anything, don't more people go to jail?"

He surveyed the class. No one seemed willing to offer an answer.

"Let's think about it for a minute," he said. "If you go to jail, you get a roof over your head and three square meals a day, and it's all free. They have TV and all sorts of recreational equipment like ping pong tables and pool tables. So, why isn't there a line of people down at the jail banging on the door to get in?"

"Well," said Becky, "there may not be any explicit costs of going to jail. But there are opportunity costs. You can't go anywhere or . . ."

"That's right," he said. "If we just looked at the explicit costs of going to jail, it might seem like a good idea. But when we take the implicit, or opportunity, costs of going to jail into account, it doesn't seem like such a hot proposition after all. The basic point here is that economists believe that you need to take *all* costs, both implicit and explicit, into account when evaluating different courses of action. There must be something to this line of reasoning, because the last time I drove past the jail there wasn't a line of people down there banging on the door to get in." Then he went to the board and wrote:

Implicit costs or opportunity costs

are the costs

of the best

foregone alternative.

"Another case where we can see the importance of distinguishing between explicit costs and opportunity costs is the cost of going to college. If you look in most college catalogues they give you cost estimates which include things like tuition and fees, room and board, books, travel, and incidentals. If we apply a little economic reasoning to the problem, we'll see that this list isn't quite correct.

"First, it isn't correct to include room and board in our list. The fact of the matter is, you'd eat and you'd want to live indoors whether you're in college or not. So, expenses for room and board aren't a part of the cost of going to college. They're one of those fixed costs that aren't important from the point of view of making the decision to go to college.

"Second, there is an important cost of going to college that doesn't show up on this list. When you're in school, you're giving up the alternative of working full time. The income you give up by not working *is* an important cost—an opportunity cost—of going to college. That's part of the reason that college graduates typically earn more than people with only a high school education. We have to compensate them for the income foregone while they were in school.

"Now, back to profits. When economists talk about profits, they're talking about the difference between total revenues and *total* costs, meaning both explicit *and* implicit costs. So economic profits are really a pure gain. It's money over and above what is needed to cover all the opportunity costs of the firm. It's the economic profits that get competed away as new firms enter the industry."

"But," said the bearded fellow, "what happens if new firms aren't able to enter the industry?"

"Well, that's a very interesting point. What you're asking, if I may be allowed to rephrase your question, is: What will happen if there are barriers to entry into the industry? In more general terms, the point you're making is that, if I change the assumptions that I'm working with, I'll arrive at a different set of conclusions. And you're right.

"In economics, all the results we derive, and all the conclusions we reach, are based on a set of premises or assumptions. If the assumptions we use are incorrect, then the results we derive and the conclusions we reach are likely to be wrong. In any kind of analysis based on logic, we have to accept the conclusions our assumptions lead us to. I think that's what Ciardi had in mind when he wrote 'A Missouri Fable.' " Then he read:

A MISSOURI FABLE
by John Ciardi

A man named Finchley once
without thinking much about
it broke into the premises of
Mr. Billy Jo Trant of these
parts, by which felonious
entry he meant to separate
Mr. Billy Jo from various
properties, but stepping on
a noise without thinking
enough about it woke Mr.
Billy Jo who took in hand a
Colt .45 and, improvising the
order of his rebuttal, fired
three times in an entirely
accurate way and then said
"Hands up!" without thinking
that the man named Finchley
once was not listening as
carefully as he might have
had Mr. Billy Jo thought to
disagree with him in a
slightly different order.

Moral: commit yourself to
another man's premises and
you may, in logic, have to
accept his conclusion.

Everyone found this funny. Eventually, however, the class settled back down.

"In Adam Smith's wonderful world, the entire economy is composed of perfectly competitive markets. You'll recall . . . ," and he went to the board and wrote:

IN A PERFECTLY COMPETITIVE MARKET:

THERE IS A LARGE NUMBER OF

INDEPENDENT BUYERS AND SELLERS;

PRODUCERS' PRODUCTS ARE IDENTICAL;

AND

THERE ARE NO BARRIERS TO ENTRY.

"Obviously, the world we live in differs from this one in many important respects. For example, in 1980, the one hundred largest manufacturing firms in the U.S. controlled about forty-seven percent of all manufacturing assets. That is an amazing figure, when you realize that there were nearly five hundred thousand manufacturing firms in the country in that year. Exxon, which is the largest manufacturing firm in the U.S., has sales that are larger than the gross national products of all but about twenty countries in the world. In fact, if Exxon were a country, it would rank right up there with Yugoslavia and Switzerland and well ahead of about one hundred twenty other countries.

"The differences between the world we live in and the competitive market system of Adam Smith are so significant that even we economists have taken note of them and developed models designed to help us understand how other types of market structures operate.

"However, it would be a mistake to dismiss what

Smith and his followers had to say out of hand. Given his assumptions, there would be a tendency for profits to be wiped out in the long run. And many, if not most, of the departures from his assumptions that we find out there in the real world are the result of conscious decisions on the part of firms, and their goal is to avoid that ironic twist of fate that Smith identified.

"One thing that firms can do to avoid the pressures of competition is to differentiate their products from those of their competitors. If their product is in some way or another unique, they will be able to exercise some control over the price. That is, they will be able to vary the price of their product without losing all their sales. This is what economists call non-price competition, and there is no shortage of it going on out there in the real world.

"The so-called 'burger wars' are an interesting case in point. We can choose between the 'flame-broiled' burgers of Burger King, the 'hot and juicy' burgers of Wendy's, and McDonald's Big Mac."

Not to mention, I thought to myself, "the Bison Burger."

"The cereal aisle at your local grocery is another interesting place to look for product differentiation. You'll find it running rampant. Choices abound, from Captain Crunch to Count Chocula and from Frankenberry to Smurf Berry Crunch, to Total to Product 19 to Special K. One of the latest, I believe, is C3-PO's, which are like two Cheerio's joined together.

"The automobile industry also provides some interesting examples. At the Ford Motor Company, where 'quality is Job 1,' you have the choice of a Thunderbird/Cougar or an Escort/Lynx. At Chrysler, where 'an American Revolution' is going on, there's the Dodge Omni/Plymouth Horizon, and Dodge Colt/Plymouth Champ. 'Nobody sweats the details like GM' and they have the

Chevy Camaro/Pontiac Firebird, the Oldsmobile Cutlass/Buick Regal, and so on.

"Then there is the Coca-Cola Bottling Company, with its famous secret formula. They make regular Coca-Cola, Diet Coca-Cola, Caffeine-Free Coca-Cola, and Diet Caffeine-Free Coca-Cola. The only bet they've missed so far is Coca-Cola-free Coca-Cola, which, as near as I can tell, would be comprised of carbonated water, caffeine, and sugar.

"Again, the goal in all these cases is to set your product apart from those of your competitors and, in so doing, isolate yourself from the pressures of price competition. If you succeed, your prize is that you'll be able to set your price high enough to turn a profit. You'll become what economists call a price-maker, as opposed to a price-taker.

"An important by-product of all this product differentiation is that the costs of engineering, market research, and advertising which it makes necessary can constitute an important barrier to entry in the industry. The week seldom passes that I don't find a plastic bag hanging on my front door with a free sample of some new shampoo or a new type of laundry detergent in it. The cost of promotional schemes like this is enormous, and the goal is simply to get a new product established.

"Another approach the modern corporation uses to reduce competitive pressures is to simply buy up competing firms. Some of the more recent examples include the Stroh Brewery Company's purchase of Schlitz and Standard Oil of California's efforts to buy the Gulf Oil Company. Then, of course, there is Texaco's purchase of Getty Oil. Earlier examples come to mind, too. Back around 1904, a fellow named William Crappo Durant decided that there might be some money to be made making cars, so he bought Buick, Cadillac, Oldsmobile, and about twenty other companies, put them all together, and named the result General Motors. The history of companies like Standard Oil and United States Steel includes similar stories of growth by merger. U.S. Steel, for example, was strung together from what had been one hundred and thirty-eight different companies, and at the time of its formation it accounted for about sixty percent of the steel production in this country. Now, of course, U.S. Steel is getting out of the steel business, since it's no longer particularly profitable. As you may know, they recently purchased Marathon Oil.

"In any event, names like *General* Motors, *Standard* Oil, and *United States* Steel give you an important clue about what the founders of these companies had on their minds. They weren't thinking small.

"Now, the models that economists use to try and take account of these departures from the competitive world of Adam Smith vary along all three of the dimensions of market structure we have identified: number of firms in the industry, types of products produced, and the ease with which new firms can enter the industry. The one thing that each of these market structures have in common is that firms in them face a downward sloping demand curve.

"Perfect competitors, you will recall, are so small that they can sell all they want at the prevailing market price. Since the products produced by firms in perfectly competitive markets are all identical, there is no way for an individual firm to raise its price and hope to sell any of its product. Buyers would simply switch to one of its competitors.

"But an imperfect competitor is in a different situation. Since each firm in an imperfectly competitive market is likely to produce a product that is slightly different from their competitors, they can raise their prices slightly without losing all their sales. Their customers develop what folks over in the marketing department call 'brand loyalty.' And, since they are likely to control a significant share of the market, they can only get people to buy more by lowering their prices. So, imperfectly competitive firms have downward sloping demand curves. As a result, they really need to have some idea about the price elasticity of demand for their products.

"The most extreme case is that of a monopoly, where there is only one firm in the industry," he said, and he wrote on the board:

IN A MONOPOLISTIC MARKET THERE IS:

A SINGLE SELLER;

A PRODUCT WITH NO CLOSE

SUBSTITUTES;

AND

ENTRY INTO THE INDUSTRY IS BARRED.

"Monopoly, translated literally, means single seller. Local gas and electric companies are cases in point. Sewer and water companies are, too.

"For an industry to be monopolized requires that entry into the industry be completely barred, and there are several different types of barriers to entry.

"One of the most effective barriers to entry is the control over some key input into the production process. For years, the DeBeer's have controlled the production of raw diamonds. As a result, they have been able to control the price of diamonds. In the early days of the telephone, American Telephone and Telegraph, or the Bell System, held control of several key patents for telecommunications equipment, and they refused to allow their manufacturing subsidiary, one Western Electric Company, to sell equipment to competing firms. As a result, they held a virtual monopoly in the telephone industry. The Aluminum Corporation of America, or Alcoa, once controlled about ninety-four percent of all the bauxite in the world, and that gave them an effective monopoly in the production of aluminum.

"Another barrier to entry is the existence of economies of scale. Economies of scale simply mean that average costs are lower for larger firms. As a result, new firms are unable to enter the market because their costs of production would be too high to allow them to effectively compete with existing firms. If economies of scale are very extensive in an industry, then it's what is known as a natural monopoly. With a natural monopoly, it simply isn't feasible to have more than one firm in the industry. Water and sewer systems are classic cases in point. How many water or sewer systems do you suppose it would make sense to have in a given geographic area?"

The answer to this question seemed obvious enough.

"Government is also credited by many economists as being a significant barrier to entry in some industries. Patents are the prime example of this, because they grant the owner exclusive rights to a product or process for seventeen years. However, there are other cases where governmental units of one sort or another act to limit entry of firms into an industry. For example, the federal government has established its own monopoly with the U.S. Postal Service by making it illegal for anyone else to carry first class mail. The federal government, acting through the Federal Reserve Bank, or the FED, limits the number of banks that operate with federal charters, and the states limit the number of banks with state charters. So, in both of these cases, the government acts as a barrier to entry into the banking industry. State licensing requirements of all kinds, for everything from doctors, lawyers, and dentists to hairdressers, barbers, and bars, are also barriers to entry into these businesses.

"When a firm is in a monopoly position, it has absolute control over the supply of a product. As a result, it is able to effectively control the price of the product by regulating the quantity it sells. And, since the monopolistic firm is the only firm in the industry, it must lower price in order to increase its sales.

"The problem with monopolies is that, left to their own devices, they will produce less, and charge much more for it than would firms in a competitive market. Their ability to control industry output lets monopolies charge higher prices and make their monopoly profits. For this reason, monopolies like gas and electric companies are regulated by some sort of public utility commission and most sewer and water systems are owned and operated by some unit of government. In other instances, government may use the antitrust laws to break up existing monopolies. The recent breakup of the telephone company is a case in point. Or, government can use its powers to prevent mergers to keep new monopolies from forming. Without some form of regulation or public control, the desire to maximize profits leads monopolists to restrict output below the level that is socially desirable in order to maintain their high prices.

"A somewhat less extreme type of market structure, and one that we encounter much more frequently than monopolies, is called a monopolistically competitive industry." Then he went to the board and wrote:

IN MONOPOLISTIC COMPETITION:

THERE IS A LARGE NUMER OF FIRMS.

THE FIRMS' PRODUCTS ARE

PARTIALLY DIFFERENTIATED,

AND

THERE ARE NO BARRIERS TO ENTRY.

"Monopolistically competitive industries have characteristics of both monopoly and perfectly competitive industries, hence the somewhat cumbersome name. The fact that each firm's product is slightly different from that of its competitors gives the firm some degree of monopoly power. The fact that a firm's product *is* different from those of other firms means that, within certain limits, the firm can vary the price of its product without losing all of its sales. So, like the case of a pure monopoly, the firm in a monopolistically competitive industry has the ability to set prices. As a result, in the short run, firms in a monopolistically competitive industry may be able to earn economic profits that exceed those a perfect competitor could have.

"The characteristic that monopolistic competition and perfect competition have in common is that there are no significant barriers to entry in either type of market. Over the long run, new firms can and will enter the industry if existing firms are making profits. So, over the long run, the competitive aspects of a monopolistically competitive industry will cause profits to be competed away.

"So, what," he asked, "would be some good examples of monopolistically competitive industries?"

"How about," replied the young man in the yellow shirt, "automobiles?"

"Well, that would depend on what part of the business you have in mind. If you're talking about the production of automobiles, it would hardly qualify. The four largest domestic car manufacturers produce about seventy-five percent of all the passenger cars sold in the U.S. In fact, these days General Motors alone accounts for around sixty percent of the sales of domestically produced cars. However, if you wanted to talk about the retail end of the business, then you'd have a pretty fair approximation of a monopolistically competitive situation. What about some other examples?"

"How about beauty salons and barber shops?" asked the redheaded woman.

"Those are pretty good cases in point, aren't they? There are a lot of them, and each tries to maintain its own special atmosphere. You've got the traditional shops, shops for the jet-setters, shops for the punk-rockers, and so forth. What are some others?"

"How about the restaurant business?" asked Becky. "There are Chinese restaurants, Mexican restaurants, Italian restaurants, Greek restaurants, health food restaurants, seafood places, steak houses, and pizza joints."

"That's a very good example. Each tries to achieve its own individuality through the type of food served and to create its own special ambience with its decor and the clothes and behavior of its staff. All the details have to mesh, from the design of the menu to the type of the furniture, to the place settings and the silverware."

He surveyed the class to see if other people had examples to offer, but no one seemed to have anything more to say.

"In point of fact," he continued, "the vast majority of

the businesses we come in contact with daily operate in monopolistically competitive markets. Grocery stores, liquor stores, bars, clothing stores, drug stores, hardware stores, shoe stores, and so on. In nearly every case, they're monopolistic competitors. In each case, you'll find a relatively large number of firms, and each firm offering a partially differentiated product."

"I don't get it," said the young man in the yellow shirt. "Grocery stores sell all different sorts of food, liquor stores sell lots of different kinds of liquor, and shoe stores have all different types of shoes. What do you mean when you say they offer partially differentiated products?"

"Well, there are a couple of things going on here. First, and foremost, retail businesses of all types offer partially differentiated products in the sense that their 'product,' if you will, is the terms and conditions under which they make their sales. Stores differ in terms of location, decor, decorum of the sales force, the way they display their products, and the like. Take shoe stores as a case in point. You've got discount shoe stores, family shoe stores, children's shoe stores, women's shoe stores, men's shoe stores, stores that specialize in athletic shoes, and who knows what else. Within each category, you've also got a wide variety in terms of the quality of shoes they sell. So, for example, there are very expensive women's shoe stores, medium-priced ones, and ones that specialize in really cheap shoes. That's what I mean when I say that retail businesses are offering partially differentiated products.

"The other point, and this is where I think you may be getting hung up, is that, in many lines of manufacture, we find a large number of small firms offering partially differentiated products. Take blue jeans as a case in point. You've got Levi's, Lee Rider, Wrangler, Calvin Klein, Gloria Vanderbilt, Jordache, J.C. Penney's Plain Pockets, and Sears Toughskins, to name only those that come most immediately to mind. Each is partially differentiated. There are differences in the way the pockets are stitched, or not stitched, in the case of Plain Pockets. Each is slightly different in terms of the way they are cut, the type of denim used to make them, and the kinds of symbols, signatures, or trademarks that appear on them. So, you can also find manufacturing firms that operate in monopolistically competitive markets. Do you see?"

"Yes. Thank you." The young man really did seem to have understood this.

"Now," the professor continued, "there are two important features of a monopolistically competitive market structure." Then he went to the board and wrote:

TWO IMPORTANT FEATURES OF

MONOPOLISTIC COMPETITION ARE:

ADVERTISING AND

OTHER FORMS OF NON-PRICE

COMPETITION

AND

EXCESS CAPACITY.

"First, let's note that in monopolistic competition, a tremendous amount of money is invested in activities aimed at differentiating one's product from that of one's competitors. Indeed, it's this very form of non-price competition that makes a monopolistically competitive market work. It shows up in the advertising and marketing budgets of these companies and in the amount of time that engineers and designers spend working on minor variations of products that serve only to differentiate one product from another.

"The other noteworthy feature is that monopolistically competitive industries tend to be characterized by excess capacity. That is, each industry tends to have too many firms operating at less than their optimal capacity. The formal proof of this is really quite nice, as you'll see later in the semester. However, it is also a concept that can be easily illustrated simply by looking at the world around you. Take, for example, barber shops. I don't know if you've ever noticed but when you walk by the typical barber shop, you'll find that the chairs are always full." He paused a moment and then said, "Full of barbers." This got a pretty good laugh.

"Another example of how monopolistically competitive industries tend to have too many firms, each operating at less than optimal capacity, is the sad case of the retail gasoline business. Back during the days of cheap gasoline, there was a station on just about every corner. In many cases more than one. In fact, there were about two hundred and twenty-six thousand gasoline stations in the United States in 1972. When the OPEC nations began increasing the price of crude oil back in 1973, gasoline prices started to rise. Rising gas prices led people to cut back on their purchases, and gasoline stations started closing right and left. By 1983, there were only around a hundred and thirty-seven thousand stations left in the whole country.

"Someone should do a study sometime of all the various things that gas stations have been converted into. Along one stretch of road in my old home town they've reappeared as everything from a record and tape store to a Mexican restaurant, a car wash, a quick oil change garage, a muffler shop, a discount tile and carpet store, and a drive-through beverage store. The fact that so many of these firms went belly-up when the demand for gas fell is really rather elegant testimony to the fact that there were too many firms in the industry in the first place.

"The final type of market structure economists identify is what is termed an oligopoly. Oligopoly, translated literally, means few sellers. In practical terms, oligopoly is a case where the industry is dominated by a few large firms. A handy rule of thumb to apply is this: If the largest four firms in the industry account for more than fifty percent of the total sales of the industry, it's an oligopoly." Then he went to the board and wrote:

IN AN OLIGOPOLY:

THERE IS A SMALL NUMBER OF LARGE

FIRMS;

EACH FIRM PRODUCES A PARTIALLY

DIFFERENTIATED PRODUCT;

AND

THERE ARE BARRIERS TO ENTRY.

"Since there are only a few large firms in an oligopolistic market, one of its most important characteristics is the interdependence of the firms in the industry. That is, the behavior of each firm has an undeniable impact on the other firms in the industry. What would be some good cases in point?"

"Well, automobile production would be one good one." Not surprisingly, it was the young man in the yellow shirt.

"Yes, that's true," said the professor. "But we already mentioned that, didn't we? What are some other examples?"

"What about the brewing industry?" asked the bearded fellow.

"Yes," said the professor. "As a matter of fact, that one is on its way to becoming a textbook example. I was looking at some figures on it the other day. It turns out that the four largest brewers, Anheuser-Busch, Miller, Strohs, and Pabst, now account for slightly more than fifty percent of all beer sales. Watching some of their antics over the past few years gives you some pretty good insights into what makes an oligopoly tick. Close your eyes for a moment and see if you can recall the jingles that go with each of their light beer commercials. Can you do it?"

"Well," said the young man in the yellow shirt indignantly, "I really don't have much time to watch TV."

"Don't you have a radio?" the professor asked. It was hard to tell if he was being serious, but I don't think he was.

"In any event," he continued, "there are a couple of lessons to be learned from the case of light beer. The first is that firms in an oligopolistic market structure can ill afford to ignore the behavior of their rivals. Once one brewer started marketing light beer, the others soon had to follow suit or risk losing a substantial part of their business. In fact, the Miller Brewing Company's rise to number two on the list is due in no small measure to the fact that the other major brewers didn't start marketing their light beers right away. They're off to the races again now with the new LA, or low alcohol, beers.

"A second point is that the introduction of all these light beers was accompanied with a tremendous amount of advertising. The same thing is true now of the new campaign for the LA beers. That's why we all, or almost all of us," and he glanced at the young man in the yellow shirt, "can hum the advertising jingles.

"A third point is that much of the advertising that goes on is really self-canceling. The reason one firm does it is because all their competitors do it. The battle is over market shares, and they can only gain at one another's expense. So the net impact of an advertising campaign might well be that you simply maintain your own share of the market. Cynics have argued that it really doesn't matter how much firms in industries like this spend on advertising, because all their ads do is cancel one another out.

"An interesting case in point here is the cigarette industry, which is also an oligopoly. Several years ago, the American Cancer Society successfully argued that they should be allowed to run public service ads following all cigarette ads on TV."

"But there are no cigarette ads on TV," said the young man in the yellow shirt.

The professor feigned surprise at this, and then said softly, "Yes, I know. But that happens later in the story.

"What happened is that the Cancer Society and the Heart and Lung Association got together and ran a really powerful series of no-smoking ads. One of my favorites had a man walking up and putting money into a cigarette machine, which immediately began making noises like a slot machine. There were whirring sounds and bells ringing and everything. The tag line was 'You Lose.'

"Now, these ads were being run *right* after the ads of the cigarette manufacturers, and they were playing the devil with their sales."

"The obvious solution, at least from the point of view of the industry as a whole, was to stop advertising their product on TV. However, no single firm could do this for fear that their rivals wouldn't stop. It was a real dilemma." Then he paused, apparently to let the dramatic tension build.

Finally, the redheaded woman asked, "So what happened?"

"The cigarette manufacturers sent their trade association to Congress to lead the fight against cigarette advertising on TV."

"So," said the young man in the yellow shirt sagely, *"that's* why there isn't any cigarette advertising on TV!"

"That's right.

"Now," the professor went on, "there are several important features of oligopolistic behavior that we should discuss." Then he went to the board and wrote:

THE IMPORTANT FEATURES

OF AN OLIGOPOLY ARE:

INTERDEPENDENCE,

THE DESIRE TO AVOID PRICE COMPETITION,

AND

PRICE LEADERSHIP PRICING.

"This interdependence of firms in an oligopolistic market extends far beyond their behavior in terms of advertising and the types of product lines they offer. Another obvious place to spot it is in terms of their pricing behavior. What you find, when you look at the issue, is that firms in oligopolistic markets absolutely abhor price competition. They'll go to tremendous lengths to avoid competing directly on the basis of price. In fact, combative advertising and the sort of product proliferation I alluded to earlier in the case of the brewing industry are prime examples of what they'll do to avoid getting into price wars.

"Their unwillingness to engage in price competition is a result of their interdependence. In fact, their interdependence leads them to be very cautious about making decisions either to raise or to lower their prices. If a single firm raises its prices, and rival firms do not, then the firm that increased its price stands to lose a substantial part of its market share. On the other hand, when a firm decides to cut its prices, it can bet that its rivals will cut their prices, too. And price cutting can easily lead to an out-and-out price war. If that happens, everyone in the industry winds up losing.

"Take the sorry story of Braniff airlines. From 1938 until 1978, airline fares were regulated by the Civil Aeronautics Board, or the CAB. So the only kind of price competition that could go on in the industry was what the CAB would sanction. When the airlines were deregulated, they no longer had the CAB to protect themselves from one another, and a price war soon broke out. It was started by Braniff.

"Eventually, air fares were cut so drastically that several airlines were on the verge of bankruptcy, and Braniff was at the front of the line. They have only recently gotten the company reorganized and back in business, and one of their first moves was to announce a whopping big fare reduction. The casual observer might begin to suspect that they're slow learners."

This prompted a few scattered chuckles from the class.

"In any event, mature oligopolies are very unlikely to enter into price wars. The automobile industry is an interesting case in point here. When auto sales need a boost, they're most likely to offer 'manufacturer's rebates' or 'below-market financing.' Either measure is, in fact, a price cut. However, both have the virtue of disguising the reality of the matter. You may have noticed that the base sticker prices of Chevrolets, Fords, and Plymouths are almost exactly the same. That's no accident.

"Another example comes to us from the ongoing 'burger wars' between McDonald's, Burger King, and Wendy's. The war is primarily the sort of advertising battle that we have come to expect. However, at one point Burger King reduced the price of their single hamburger to thirty-nine cents and McDonald's promptly followed. This caused analysts to suspect that a price war would soon break out, and prices of the stock of both companies dropped several points. The moral of the story here is that everyone who understands much about the matter *knows* that direct price competition is bad news.

"The upshot is that prices of oligopolistic firms tend to be sticky. That is, fear of the consequences of raising or lowering prices leads firms in these industries to keep prices pretty much where they are.

"However, periodically, the need to increase prices does arise. In that case, the mature oligopoly will engage in what is known as price leadership pricing. What happens is that one firm that has, over time, become the acknowledged price leader, will announce a price increase. Shortly thereafter, all the other firms in the industry will announce their price increases. The best place to see this, or at least the place you can see it most often, is in banks' announcements of changes in their prime interest rates. One bank announces its increase in the morning, a couple of others follow in the afternoon. By the next day, they're up all across the country. Another place you can spot it is in the annual announcements of price increases by the auto companies. GM will come out with its price lists on Monday, and all the others will follow on Tuesday and Wednesday. Or, sometimes Ford gets to go first and all the others follow."

Then he paused for a moment, glanced at his watch, and surveyed the class.

"Well, that's enough for today. We've had a pretty fair overview of the things a manager needs to know about microeconomics. For class on Wednesday, read the first three chapters of Baumol's *Economic Theory and Operations Analysis.* Good day."

I walked to the front of the room and stood by as he collected his notes. The young man in the yellow shirt asked whether it would be possible to use an earlier edition of the text, and a couple of other students had questions about whether research projects would be required and how to go about dropping other courses and adding his.

Finally, he finished with their questions, turned to me, and said, "Well, Bob, did you get all that?"

"Yes sir, I think so," I said. "The one thing that confuses me a little is all this business about different types of market structures."

He appeared to think about this for a minute. Then said, "The point is that managers need to know about the structure of the industry they're operating in if they are going to make intelligent decisions. The sort of marketing strategy a firm will follow depends a lot on the type of market structure the firm operates in.

"Firms in markets that approximate perfectly competitive conditions don't have any control over prices, but they can control the timing of their sales. Farmers and people who play the stock market are both good cases in point. For both, a lot hinges on making good decisions about when to buy and when to sell. In these instances the cardinal rule of speculation really holds sway."

"The cardinal rule of speculation?" I asked. "What's that?"

"Buy low, sell high," he said. If he was surprised that I hadn't known that, he did a good job of hiding it.

"Now, in monopolistically competitive markets the

key is making good pricing decisions. Which is to say that you really have to have some idea about what the demand for your product looks like. Most firms in these types of markets don't have the resources to hire economists and market researchers to get that sort of information for them, and the result is that a lot of them wind up going broke.

"In reality, it's only the large firms which, for the most part, operate in oligopolistic markets, who have the money to employ economists and marketing people. They're the ones that are in the best position to gather and interpret the data that are necessary to try to find the profit maximizing price and output, where marginal revenue equals marginal cost. And, sadly enough, even they are wrong a lot of the time.

"What most small businesses wind up doing, consciously or unconsciously, is simply calculating their break-even points—that is, the level of output where total revenue exceeds total costs. Then they try and produce and sell in that range. If they can do that, it will be profitable for them.

"As I said in class, firms in these oligopolistic market structures rarely compete on the basis of price. Competition there centers on advertising, product differentiation, and service. In fact, this is one of the main points the fellows who wrote *In Search of Excellence* made. Some large firms had lost sight of the importance of service, until the Japanese reminded them of it. That's one of the reasons the book has been so popular.

"Does that clear things up some for you?"

"Yes, sir, it does. Thank you." I really was beginning to feel like I had a pretty good grasp of it.

"Good. There is only one little piece of business left to wrap up. Come on back over to my office and we'll discuss what every manager needs to know about international economics."

3

What Every Manager Needs to Know about International Economics

"Now, there is one other area we need to think about. In some respects, for a young person like you, international economics may be the most important thing of all for you to understand," he said, relighting the ever-present pipe and leaning back in his chair.

"There was a time—not too long ago—when it was all relatively simple. One of the few things almost all economists agree on is that free trade between countries benefits everybody. Even the most myopic members of Congress can understand that it is more efficient for bananas to be grown in Central America than it would be for us to try and grow them in greenhouses here. So we grow wheat and trade it to Central America for bananas, and the obvious result is that we all have more bananas *and* more wheat. This, as you probably know, is called the *theory of comparative advantage*, which simply posits that if everyone does whatever they can do most efficiently, then everyone gains. Perhaps, just to make sure we've got it straight, you should make a note of it."

THE THEORY OF COMPARATIVE ADVANTAGE DEMONSTRATES THAT EVERYONE GAINS WHEN COUNTRIES SPECIALIZE IN WHAT THEY CAN DO MOST EFFICIENTLY AND TRADE THE RESULTING PRODUCTS FOR THINGS THEY CANNOT PRODUCE EFFICIENTLY.

"Now, if that were all there was to it then you could go on home and I could watch 'General Hospital.' The problem is that history has not been very kind to this relatively obvious truth. That's why understanding history is crucial to understanding today's reality. This, I presume you are beginning to realize, is often the case. The problem is that exports create jobs just like consumption, investment, and government spending do, as we saw this morning. So, since everyone wants jobs, the game becomes one of trying to export more than the other fellow. If you are successful at this, then you are shipping more goods out of the country than you are importing in. This means you have less goods for home consumption, but you have more jobs. Which is a curious trade-off I have always thought, but it has been every nation's policy for quite a while now."

"Excuse me, sir." I was getting confused. "If we export more than we import, how do the other countries pay for it?"

"That is a good question. If they are going to buy our goods, then they have to have dollars to pay for them, don't they? Again, you have to understand the history involved. In the 'good old days' this was all handled by gold. If a country imported more than it exported, then it had to make up the difference by coming up with the gold to pay for it. That is, countries used gold to cover their balance of payments deficits. But, by the end of World War II, when the Allies gathered at Bretton Woods to restructure the international monetary system, it was becoming obvious to everyone that this was a bit of a cumbersome system. So, it was decided that, since we in the U.S. had, at the time, most of the world's gold supply, we would just make the dollar redeemable in gold at any country's demand. That way, the dollar was 'as good as gold' and everyone could simply use dollars to settle international claims and everything would be a lot simpler all around. So write this down:"

THE BRETTON WOODS AGREEMENT,

IN ESSENCE,

MADE THE U.S. DOLLAR

THE INTERNATIONAL CURRENCY.

ALMOST ALL INTERNATIONAL TRANSACTIONS

AFTER THAT WERE,

AND STILL ARE,

DENOMINATED IN DOLLARS.

"Actually, this was a case of simply applying the Golden Rule: 'Whoever has the gold makes the rules,' because what it really did was excuse the U.S. from the traditional discipline of international finance. Which meant that, in reality, as long as the rest of the world would accept dollars as payment we could run balance of payments deficits any time we wanted to. It's like the President's checking account. People never send the checks in for collection because they want to keep the autograph. So he can spend whatever he wants without having to worry about balancing his checkbook."

"So we would spend whatever we wanted to without having to balance our budget internationally . . .," I started to say when he interrupted me.

"That's right. And, it worked pretty well for a while. It allowed us to give away a lot of money in foreign aid, which came back to us when it was used to purchase products here. That is, it created jobs for us, which is what foreign aid always does. And it allowed us to maintain troops around the world and fight a couple of wars and so on. But, by the late sixties, it was becoming obvious to everyone that we couldn't make good on our pledge to redeem dollars held by other countries in gold. Our gold supply was down to some ten billion, and the dollars outstanding totaled more than fifty billion. President Nixon, among others, was getting a little worried about this, so in August of 1971 he simply 'shut the gold window,' as they say—canceled our pledge to exchange gold for dollars. This left the rest of the world holding fifty billion dollars that were now worth nothing, unless you wanted to spend them to buy U.S. products. This is crucial to understanding the rest of the story, so perhaps you had better write it down."

IN AUGUST OF 1971,

THE UNITED STATES

CANCELED ITS PLEDGE

TO REDEEM DOLLARS FOR GOLD.

THIS HAD THE NET EFFECT

OF DE-MONETIZING GOLD

AND MAKING IT LIKE ANY

OTHER COMMODITY THAT

IS TRADED IN THE MARKETPLACE

AND PRICED ACCORDING TO

SUPPLY AND DEMAND.

"So, these days, gold really has nothing to do with the monetary system at all, except in the sense that its market price serves as a good 'inflation barometer.' You'll note, if you look at the data, that the price of gold tends to rise as inflation rates get higher and vice versa.

"But, there's more. Since the U.S. economy is the strongest in the world, most people accepted this as a necessary move to keep international trade moving. In fact, these days there are something like one trillion dollars held abroad; *Eurodollars* they are called, as you probably know. But the significance of all this is that, from that time on, the economies of almost all other countries in the world were tied to the U.S. economy. So, since virtually all international transactions—exchanges of goods and services—are in dollars, everyone now has a stake in what happens in the U.S. economy. That's why the whole world gets nervous when our inflation rate gets high. The value of the dollars they are holding decreases, just as happens to you and me.

"A related, but even more important, aspect of this concerns what happens to interest rates. As you may remember, I said this morning that interest rates are crucial to everything that has to do with the economy. Internationally that's even more true.

"The reason is that interest rates around the world tend to be the same as they are in the United States. Suppose, for example, that you are an investor in London and you can get a ten percent return by investing in bonds there, but you can get twelve percent by investing in New York. What would you do?"

"I would make the investment in New York," I said, feeling better.

"And how, exactly, would you do that?"

"Well, I guess I would give the money to my broker and tell him to invest it in New York."

"And what, exactly, would he have to do?"

"Well, ah, I'm not sure," I said, knowing I was losing it again.

"Obviously, he would have to take your money—which would be in British pounds sterling—and exchange it for dollars. Then he could make the bond purchase in New York. And you would have a debt instrument which paid you twelve percent interest in dollars. If this were happening all around the world, what would the result be?"

"There would be an increase in the demand for dollars?" I ventured.

"Good enough. It would, indeed. So the net result of high interest rates in the United States is a strong dollar abroad. Which means our exports are more expensive, but our imports are cheaper. So, again, we can import more than we export, and the difference is covered by the in-flow of dollars from other countries looking for higher interest rates. Of course, we lose jobs from this since we export less, but we gain cheaper imports, which helps keep our inflation rate down. So, let's say you are the manager of a multinational corporation. How do you deal with this?"

"I guess I would try to shift as many of my purchases to other countries as I could. I mean I would buy imported products since they would be cheaper."

"Exactly. So, what is the net result of high interest rates in the U.S.?"

I was beginning to get the picture. "High interest rates attract foreign funds here, but this makes the dollar strong. In turn we lose jobs as imports are increased."

"Right. So high interest rates discourage investment here and in a roundabout way encourage it abroad. So we lose on both counts. Perhaps you'd better make a note of this."

HIGH INTEREST RATES:

DISCOURAGE DOMESTIC INVESTMENT,

AND CAUSE THE VALUE

OF THE DOLLAR TO RISE.

THIS INCREASES IMPORTS,

AND DECREASES EXPORTS,

WHICH COSTS US JOBS.

ALL OF THIS ALLOWS US TO RUN

BALANCE OF PAYMENTS DEFICITS,

WHICH ARE FINANCED BY INVESTMENTS

FROM ABROAD.

All I have to do, I was thinking as I wrote it down, is keep track of all that.

Then he said, "All you have to do, if you manage a multinational corporation, is keep track of all that and one other point. Recently, say, in the last ten years or so, there have been some dramatic changes taking place in the world of international finance, and they are complicated. So complicated, in fact, that some say there are only twenty or so people in the world who really understand what is going on. However, . . ."

He smiled again.

" . . . since I am one of those twenty people, we'll be O.K. What happened—as I mentioned at lunch—was that the OPEC countries decided to raise the price of oil by some seventeen hundred percent. What resulted was the largest transfer of wealth in history. Hundreds of billions of dollars were transferred from the Western world to the essentially impoverished Arab countries. That is, they sent us the oil and we sent them the dollars to pay for it. Now what, as a practical matter, do you suppose they did with those dollars, which amounted to far more than they could ever spend?"

"Well, I guess they started a savings account or something like that." How was I supposed to know?

"Right, Robert. But where? Where would you start a savings account if you won the lottery tomorrow?"

"I guess in the bank that I thought was the most risk-free and where I could get the highest interest."

"And, assuming you are sitting in, say, Saudi Arabia surveying the world, where would that be? Obviously, you would put your money in the strongest bank in the strongest country in the world. And that, of course, would be some large bank right here in the U.S.A. So the Arab countries re-deposited those dollars right back here in New York. Hundreds of billions, remember.

"Now, next question: If you are a banker, how do you earn your money?"

I knew the answer to that one. It was the only thing I remembered from the money and banking class. "Banks take in deposits from one customer and pay the lowest rate of interest possible and then loan it out to another customer at the highest rate they can get. The difference is their profit."

"O.K. Now, assume you are a banker sitting on several hundred billion dollars worth of deposits from the OPEC countries. What are you going to do with all that money? Obviously, you are going to try to lend it out somewhere. In fact, not only are you going to *try* to, but you *have* to. Otherwise you'll be out of business.

"So, what the banks did was look around for the highest rate of return and aggressively lend out the Arab oil deposits. And, since the U.S. economy was in a recession in mid-seventies, there wasn't much demand for loans here. But the banks soon discovered that the Third World countries, all of whom are short of capital, were only too happy to borrow the money. And that's where much of it went, mostly to Latin America, especially Argentina, Brazil, and Mexico. So, it's an interesting cycle when you stop and think about it."

He stopped and sketched something on the back of another envelope, and handed it to me. I was beginning to wonder if he ever used regular paper.

"We call it recycling of petro-dollars.

"Does that make any sense to you?" he asked, leaning back and lighting his pipe again as if he were expecting a long answer.

"Yes, sir, it does. It also seems to be a logical way to transfer the money to where it's needed."

"Well, it does make sense, except for two minor problems, one of which, it seems to me, could have been

RECYCLING PETRO-DOLLARS

predicted. The other, perhaps not. The first is that many of the Third World countries who were borrowing these funds and using them for their own development were also benefiting from the high price of oil. Mexico and Nigeria are two of the more obvious examples. Everyone assumed that they were good credit risks, since they could use their own oil revenues to pay back the loans. But what no one realized until it was too late was that the OPEC countries had incorrectly estimated the price elasticity of demand for oil—a concept we discussed this afternoon in class, as you no doubt recall. They assumed that the demand for oil was inelastic; i.e., that we would buy it at any price, overlooking the fact that, when prices get high enough, people will find ways to reduce their consumption. They'll car pool, take the bus, dial down their thermostats, insulate their houses, weatherstrip their doors and windows, and whatever else it takes to reduce their energy expenditures. All these things actually happened, and the result was that the bottom fell out of the oil market and oil prices fell. Falling oil prices eliminated much of the expected revenues, not only for the OPEC countries but, more importantly, for the now heavily in debt oil-producing Third World countries."

"So, in a way, petro-dollar recycling boomeranged," I said. This was getting interesting.

"Well, as we shall see in a minute, that is putting it a bit mildly. The other thing everyone overlooked was the simple effects of compounding. The bankers, one would think, should have known better. But apparently, they didn't. Let me illustrate with a simple example.

"Let's assume that a country, say, Mexico, is borrowing five hundred million dollars a year from U.S. banks and that, just to keep this simple, they are paying twenty percent a year interest. Also, for simplicity, we'll assume that they are getting the loans under the most favorable possible condition: no principal payments are required, only interest. And let's also assume that this all started about the same time as the petro-dollar recycling did, say, 1973. Under these conditions, what kind of shape do you think the Mexican economy would be in now?"

"Well, I don't know exactly, sir. I guess if they invested the money in something that gave them a return of more than twenty percent, they should be better off."

"This is certainly true, I suppose. Have you paid any attention to what is happening to the Mexican economy lately? Their economic growth rate has been negative for the past several years. In '83 it was a *minus* five percent, while their population growth rate has been running at a *positive* three percent. That means that people in Mexico—on average—became eight percent worse off during that year. And, on top of that, they now owe around ninety billion dollars to foreign banks, which is almost as much as their total gross national product. How do you suppose they got in such shape?"

"Well, it must be complicated," I said. I was learning that he liked that word. At any rate, I didn't have the foggiest idea.

"It is, indeed, Robert. It is, indeed. So complicated, in fact, that even I can't think of a simple way to explain it."

He smiled again. And so did I, not knowing what else to do. Then he started typing something on the computer terminal on his desk. To my amazement, figures started appearing on the screen of the TV in the corner, or what I had thought was a TV.

"Just look at this. If the Mexicans are paying twenty percent interest, that means that by the sixth year they pay as much *interest* as they get in new loans. And if you carry this out a bit further you can see that, by the eleventh year, they are paying more total interest than they have received in total loans. After that it's all down-

ANNUAL LOAN OF 500 MILLION
ASSUMING NO PRINCIPAL REPAYMENT
(in millions)

YEAR	NEW LOAN	ANNUAL INTEREST	TOTAL LOAN	TOTAL INTEREST PAID
1	500	—	500	—
2	500	100	1000	100
3	500	200	1500	300
4	500	300	2000	600
5	500	400	2500	1000
6	500*	500*	3000	1500
7	500	600	3500	2100
8	500	700	4000	2800
9	500	800	4500	3600
10	500	900	5000	4500
11	500	1000	5500**	5500**
12	500	1100	6000	6600

*After 5 years, annual interest = new loans.
**By the eleventh year, total interest due begins to exceed total loans.

hill, or perhaps I should say, uphill. The result of this process is that after a few years there is a net flow of funds out of the country, which tends to get worse and worse. Obviously, this is a bit of an oversimplification, but, in fact, almost any kind of foreign investment has the same effect. If you don't believe me, take a look at the Mexican balance of payments data sometime. Or any Third World debtor for that matter."

"But how can they keep this up?"

"They can borrow more money, which, of course, just makes the situation worse, or they can increase their exports, or decrease their imports. None of which is a very feasible solution. In the Mexican case they have decreased their imports, which, since their economy is very dependent on U.S. technology, has just made the situation worse. As things presently stand, they would have no option but to borrow more money and simply 'roll over,' as we say, the debt. And, interestingly enough, the banks don't have much option but to loan them the money to do it. There is an old saying: 'If you owe a bank a thousand dollars and can't pay it, you're in trouble. If you owe a bank a million dollars and can't pay it, the bank is in trouble.' And the banks are, indeed, in serious trouble because of all this."

"But doesn't that just make everything worse, as all this keeps compounding?"

"Robert, you are beginning to get the picture," he said, and smiled. "The international monetary system is now facing one of its worst crises ever, and if you should end up being a manager for a corporation that does business internationally, you had better keep on top of it. And you can't do that unless you understand it, which, I presume, you now do.

"There are now some eight hundred billion dollars in loans outstanding to Third World countries, and virtually none of them are repaying principal. Most, in fact, can't even pay the interest. That, my friend, is a problem. It is so serious that I am certainly glad I decided to become a teacher instead of a banker, which was one of my options a few years back. Have you ever considered going into teaching, Robert?"

"Well, no, sir, but it is beginning to look more attractive all the time."

"I think that about covers it. Do you have any more questions?"

"I guess not, sir. I must say, this has been a very interesting day . . ."

"Do you have your notes?" he asked.

"Yes, sir," I said, as I pulled out my pad.

"How about reading them back to me?"

Somehow I knew this was going to happen. I flipped back to the first page and began reading:

———

THERE ARE THREE AREAS OF ECONOMICS

EVERY MANAGER SHOULD UNDERSTAND:

MACRO, MICRO, AND INTERNATIONAL.

"And," I said, "then we started talking about macro-economics."

———

SINCE WAGES TEND NOT
TO BE FLEXIBLE DOWNWARD,
UNEMPLOYMENT IS THE GENERAL CASE.

■

ROBOTS CAN MAKE
AN AUTOMOBILE, BUT
THEY WILL NEVER
BUY ONE.

———

GOVERNMENT CONTROLS THE ECONOMY
BY INFLUENCING THE OVERALL LEVEL
OF
CONSUMER EXPENDITURES,
INVESTMENT EXPENDITURES,
AND GOVERNMENT EXPENDITURES.

———

INVESTMENT BEHAVIOR DEPENDS
ON INTEREST RATES.
IN FACT, ALMOST EVERYTHING
DEPENDS ON INTEREST RATES.
HIGH INTEREST RATES
DISCOURAGE INVESTMENT;
LOW INTEREST RATES
ENCOURAGE INVESTMENT.

■

THE FEDERAL RESERVE BANK
CAN INFLUENCE INVESTMENT
BY CHANGING INTEREST RATES.

———

To INCREASE THE LEVEL
OF ECONOMIC ACTIVITY,
INCREASE GOVERNMENT EXPENDITURES
OR
DECREASE TAXES.
To DECREASE THE LEVEL
OF ECONOMIC ACTIVITY,
DECREASE GOVERNMENT
EXPENDITURES
OR
INCREASE TAXES.

———

ONCE THE ECONOMY IS AT
FULL EMPLOYMENT
WE MUST KEEP
SAVINGS AND TAXES EQUAL TO
GOVERNMENT EXPENDITURES
AND INVESTMENT.
ANY VARIATION FROM THIS
WILL CAUSE INFLATION OR
UNEMPLOYMENT.

———

ESSENTIALLY, THE ECONOMY IS
CONTROLLED BY
THE FEDERAL GOVERNMENT,
WITH FISCAL POLICY
—TAXES AND EXPENDITURES—
AND BY
THE FEDERAL RESERVE BANK,
WITH MONETARY POLICY
—THE MONEY SUPPLY
AND INTEREST RATES.
THE WAY THESE TOOLS ARE USED
DEPENDS ON THE GOALS OF
THE ADMINISTRATION IN POWER.

——

MACROECONOMICS EXPLAINS HOW YOU CAN CONTROL THE TRADE-OFF BETWEEN UNEMPLOYMENT AND INFLATION.

"And then," I said, pausing to catch my breath, "in your class I took these notes."

———

PROFITS

EQUAL

TOTAL REVENUES

MINUS

TOTAL COSTS.

■

IF COSTS DON'T CHANGE

AS OUTPUT CHANGES, THEN

TO MAXIMIZE PROFITS

SIMPLY MAXIMIZE TOTAL REVENUE.

———

PRICE ELASTIC DEMAND:
PERCENTAGE CHANGE IN QUANTITY DEMANDED
IS GREATER THAN
PERCENTAGE CHANGE IN PRICE.

■

PRICE INELASTIC DEMAND:
PERCENTAGE CHANGE IN QUANTITY DEMANDED
IS LESS THAN
PERCENTAGE CHANGE IN PRICE.

———

IF IT LOOMS LARGE IN THE BUDGET

OR HAS LOTS OF SUBSTITUTES,

ITS DEMAND IS PROBABLY ELASTIC.

DECREASE PRICE TO INCREASE REVENUES.

■

IF IT DOESN'T COST MUCH

OR HAS VERY FEW SUBSTITUTES,

ITS DEMAND IS PROBABLY INELASTIC.

INCREASE PRICE TO INCREASE REVENUES.

WHEN COSTS VARY WITH OUTPUT,
MAXIMIZING PROFITS
MEANS FINDING THE OUTPUT LEVEL
WHERE THE DIFFERENCE BETWEEN
TOTAL REVENUE AND TOTAL COST
IS GREATEST.

———

VARIABLE COSTS
ARE COSTS TO CONSIDER
IN MAKING DECISIONS
ABOUT WHAT LEVEL OF OUTPUT
TO PRODUCE.

———

AVERAGE COST
IS TOTAL COST
DIVIDED BY TOTAL OUTPUT.

■

MARGINAL COST
IS THE *CHANGE* IN
TOTAL COST
DUE TO A
CHANGE IN OUTPUT.

———

TO MAXIMIZE PROFITS,
PRODUCE WHERE
MARGINAL REVENUE
EQUALS
MARGINAL COST.

■

IT MAKES ECONOMIC SENSE
TO PURSUE ANY ACTIVITY
UP TO THE POINT WHERE
THE MARGINAL BENEFIT OF IT
EQUALS
ITS MARGINAL COST.

——

IMPLICIT COSTS OR OPPORTUNITY COSTS
ARE THE COSTS
OF THE BEST
FOREGONE ALTERNATIVE.

———

IN A PERFECTLY COMPETITIVE MARKET:
THERE IS A LARGE NUMBER OF
INDEPENDENT BUYERS AND SELLERS;
PRODUCERS' PRODUCTS ARE IDENTICAL;
AND
THERE ARE NO BARRIERS TO ENTRY.

■

IN A MONOPOLISTIC MARKET THERE IS:
A SINGLE SELLER;
A PRODUCT WITH NO CLOSE
SUBSTITUTES;
AND
ENTRY INTO THE INDUSTRY IS BARRED.

———

IN MONOPOLISTIC COMPETITION:
THERE IS A LARGE NUMBER OF FIRMS.
THE FIRMS' PRODUCTS ARE
PARTIALLY DIFFERENTIATED,
AND
THERE ARE NO BARRIERS TO ENTRY.
■

TWO IMPORTANT FEATURES OF
MONOPOLISTIC COMPETITION ARE:
ADVERTISING AND
OTHER FORMS OF NON-PRICE
COMPETITION
AND
EXCESS CAPACITY.

—

IN AN OLIGOPOLY:

THERE IS A SMALL NUMBER OF LARGE FIRMS;

EACH FIRM PRODUCES A PARTIALLY

DIFFERENTIATED PRODUCT;

AND

THERE ARE BARRIERS TO ENTRY.

■

THE IMPORTANT FEATURES

OF AN OLIGOPOLY ARE:

INTERDEPENDENCE,

THE DESIRE TO AVOID PRICE COMPETITION,

AND

PRICE LEADERSHIP PRICING.

"And, finally, we discussed international economics."

———

THE THEORY OF COMPARATIVE
ADVANTAGE
DEMONSTRATES THAT EVERYONE GAINS
WHEN COUNTRIES SPECIALIZE
IN WHAT THEY CAN DO MOST
EFFICIENTLY AND
TRADE THE RESULTING PRODUCTS
FOR THINGS THEY CANNOT
PRODUCE EFFICIENTLY.

———

THE BRETTON WOODS AGREEMENT,

IN ESSENCE,

MADE THE U.S. DOLLAR

THE INTERNATIONAL CURRENCY.

ALMOST ALL INTERNATIONAL TRANSACTIONS

AFTER THAT WERE,

AND STILL ARE,

DENOMINATED IN DOLLARS.

———

IN AUGUST OF 1971,
THE UNITED STATES
CANCELED ITS PLEDGE
TO REDEEM DOLLARS FOR GOLD.
THIS HAD THE NET EFFECT
OF DE-MONETIZING GOLD
AND MAKING IT LIKE ANY
OTHER COMMODITY THAT
IS TRADED IN THE MARKETPLACE
AND PRICED ACCORDING TO
SUPPLY AND DEMAND.

———

HIGH INTEREST RATES:
DISCOURAGE DOMESTIC INVESTMENT;
AND CAUSE THE VALUE
OF THE DOLLAR TO RISE.
THIS INCREASES IMPORTS,
AND DECREASES EXPORTS,
WHICH COSTS US JOBS.
ALL OF THIS ALLOWS US TO RUN
BALANCE OF PAYMENTS DEFICITS,
WHICH ARE FINANCED BY INVESTMENTS
FROM ABROAD.

"How long did that take?"

"Just a few minutes."

"Very good, Robert. It looks like we've created an *instant economist*. Come back and see me again in a few years. By then you will really understand why all this is important. And give my regards to your father."

"I will, indeed, sir. And thanks again for your time." By then he had flipped a switch on the TV and was lighting his pipe again. "General Hospital" was just beginning. I let myself out quietly.

Epilogue

I knew I should be getting home. I did, after all, have a job interview in the morning. But I just couldn't make myself pass up Joe's Campus Bar. It was crowded and Michael Jackson's "Thriller" blared from the jukebox. I ordered a beer and surveyed the scene. An old habit.

There, at a corner table, were several graduate students from Professor Marshall's class—including Becky. They were talking animatedly about something and I hesitated about joining them. Somehow, I had to think of an opening. I pulled out my notes. There it was: To maximize profits, produce where marginal revenue equals marginal cost. Maybe this evening would end up being as interesting as the day had been. With all the composure I could muster, I walked over to the table.

"Hi," I said to Becky. "I'm Bob Smith, the guy who sat in on Professor Marshall's class, remember?"

"Sure. How ya' doing?"

"Oh, I'm fine. Ah . . . you know, I haven't had all that much economics before, and I was wondering, Becky, if you could help me with this one thing?"

"Well, that depends."

"It's this marginal revenue and marginal cost thing. I'm not sure I really understand it."

"Oh, that. It's really quite simple." She pulled a strangely familiar-looking envelope out of her purse and said, "It goes like this—"

$$\text{IF } \pi = R(Q) - C(Q)$$

$$\text{THEN MAX OF } \pi \text{ IS}$$

$$\frac{d\pi}{dQ} = \frac{dR}{dQ} - \frac{dC}{dQ}$$

$$\text{OR}$$

$$MR = \frac{dR}{dQ} = \frac{dC}{dQ} = MC$$

$$\text{IF (AND ONLY IF)}$$

$$\frac{d^2\pi}{dQ^2} = \frac{d^2R}{dQ^2} - \frac{d^2C}{dQ^2} < 0$$

I got up from the table, trying desperately to somehow regain my composure, and stammered, "Well, maybe I could call you sometime. But I'm afraid I didn't catch your last name."

"Marshall. Becky Marshall," she said.

FURTHER READING

Anyone who might wish to pursue the details of all this will find the following readable and instructive.

Economics: A Tool for Understanding Society by Tom Riddell, Jean Shackelford, and Stephen Stamos, Jr. (Addison-Wesley, 3d ed., 1985) is a refreshingly lucid and painless treatment of the entire spectrum. The study guide that accompanies it, *Studying and Thinking about Economics and Society* by John Charles Pool (Addison-Wesley, 1985), is written in the same vein.

The history of it all is treated in a very readable fashion in Robert Heilbroner's *The Worldly Philosophers* (Simon & Schuster, 1980); and you can find the conservative view persuasively argued in Milton Friedman's *Capitalism and Freedom* (University of Chicago Press, 1962).

In addition, one can find the party line on economic policy explained in detail annually in *The Economic Report of the President* available from the U.S. Government Printing Office. Some other recent works that treat various aspects of the topic in a readable manner are: *Dangerous Currents* by Lester Thurow (Random House, 1983), *An Inquiry into the Poverty of Economics* by Kenneth Jameson and Charles Wilbur (University of Notre Dame Press, 1983), and *The Next American Frontier* by Robert Reich (Times Books, 1983). The international sector is amusingly explained by Adam Smith (a.k.a. George Goodman) in *Paper Money* (Summit Books, 1981) and in a more up-to-date version, *Debt Shock* by Darrell Delamaide (Doubleday, 1984).